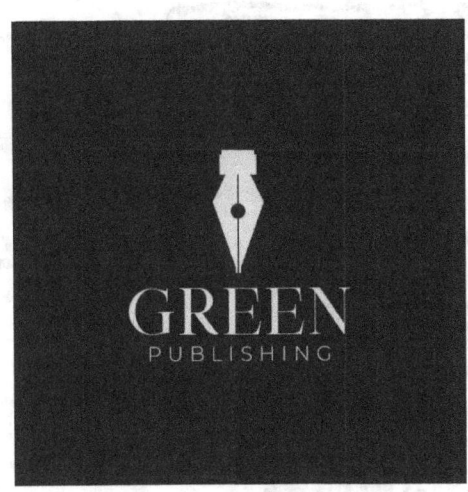

Green Publishing
Copyright © 2021 by Devan Brie S. Green

All rights reserved, including the right of reproduction in any form.

ISBN: 9798759023234

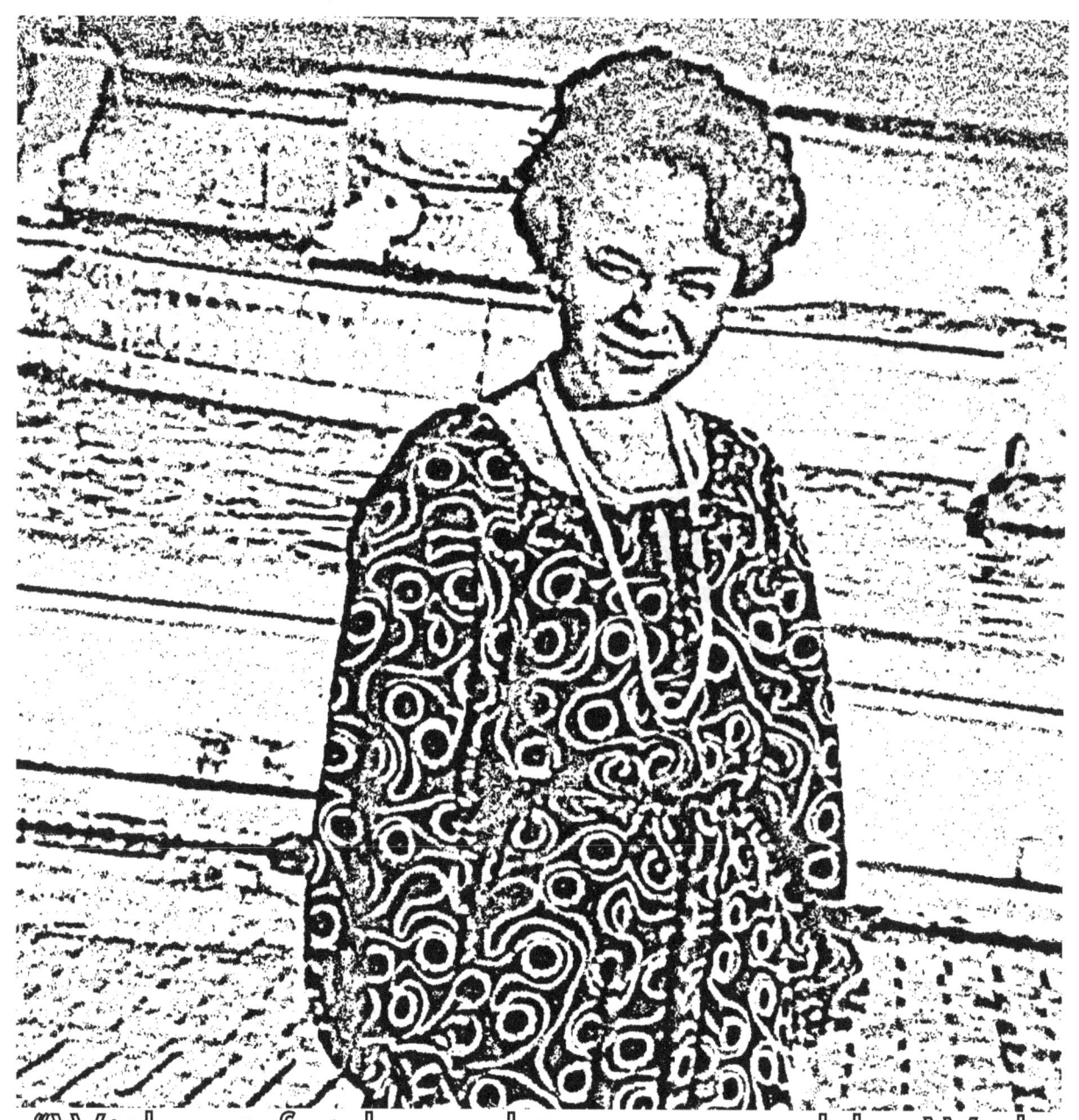

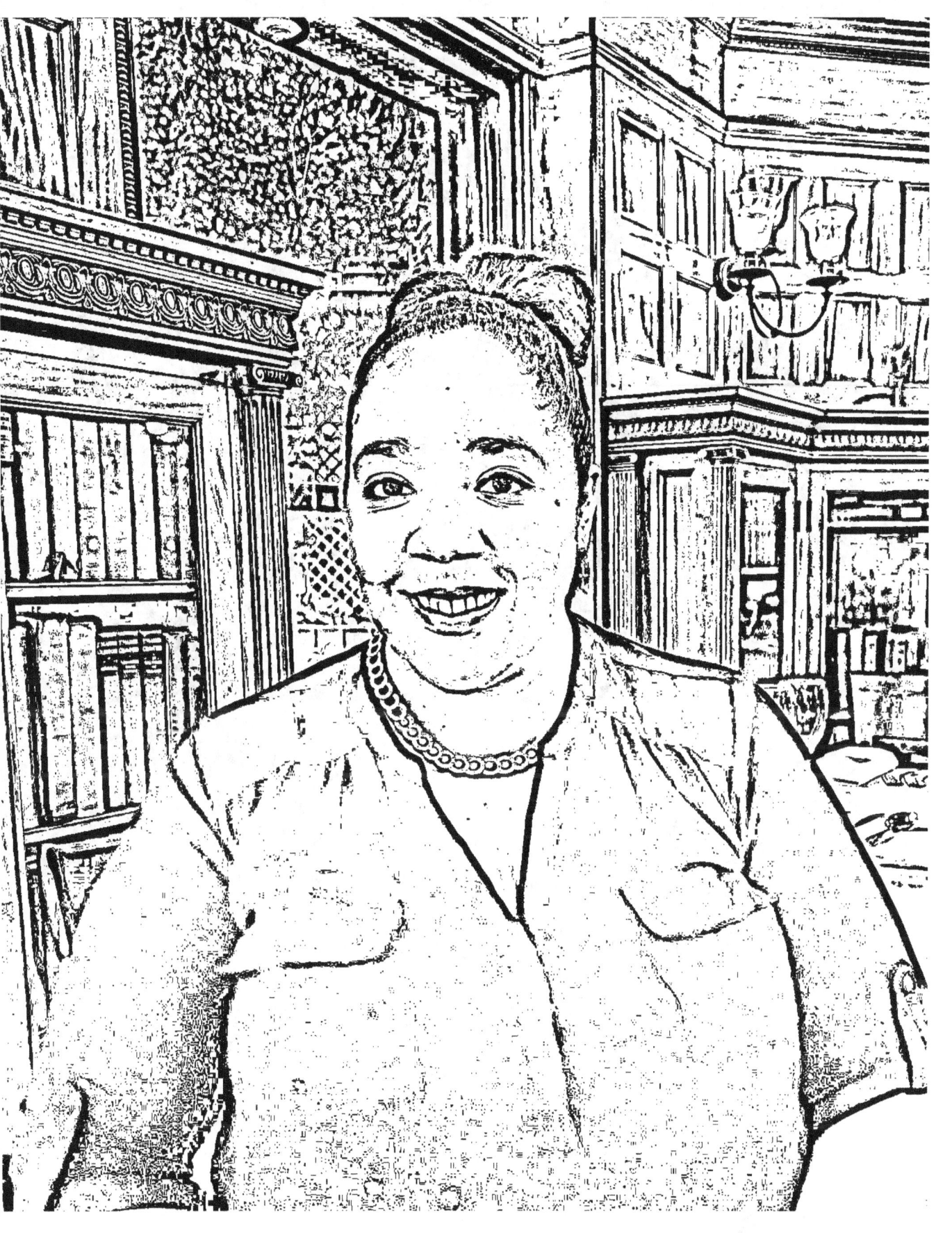

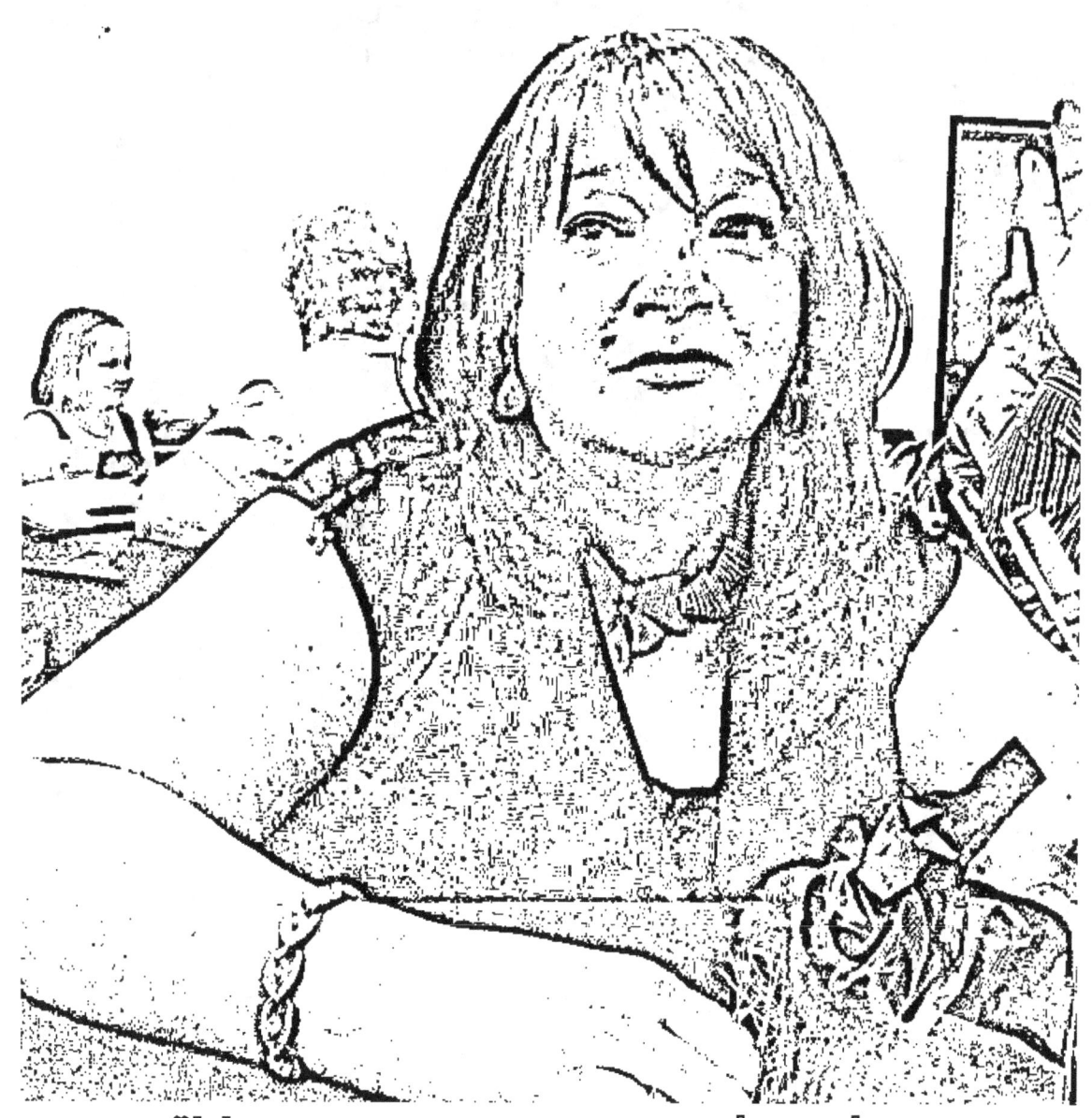

"Hate is too great a burden to bear. It injures the hater more than it injures the hated."
—Coretta Scott King

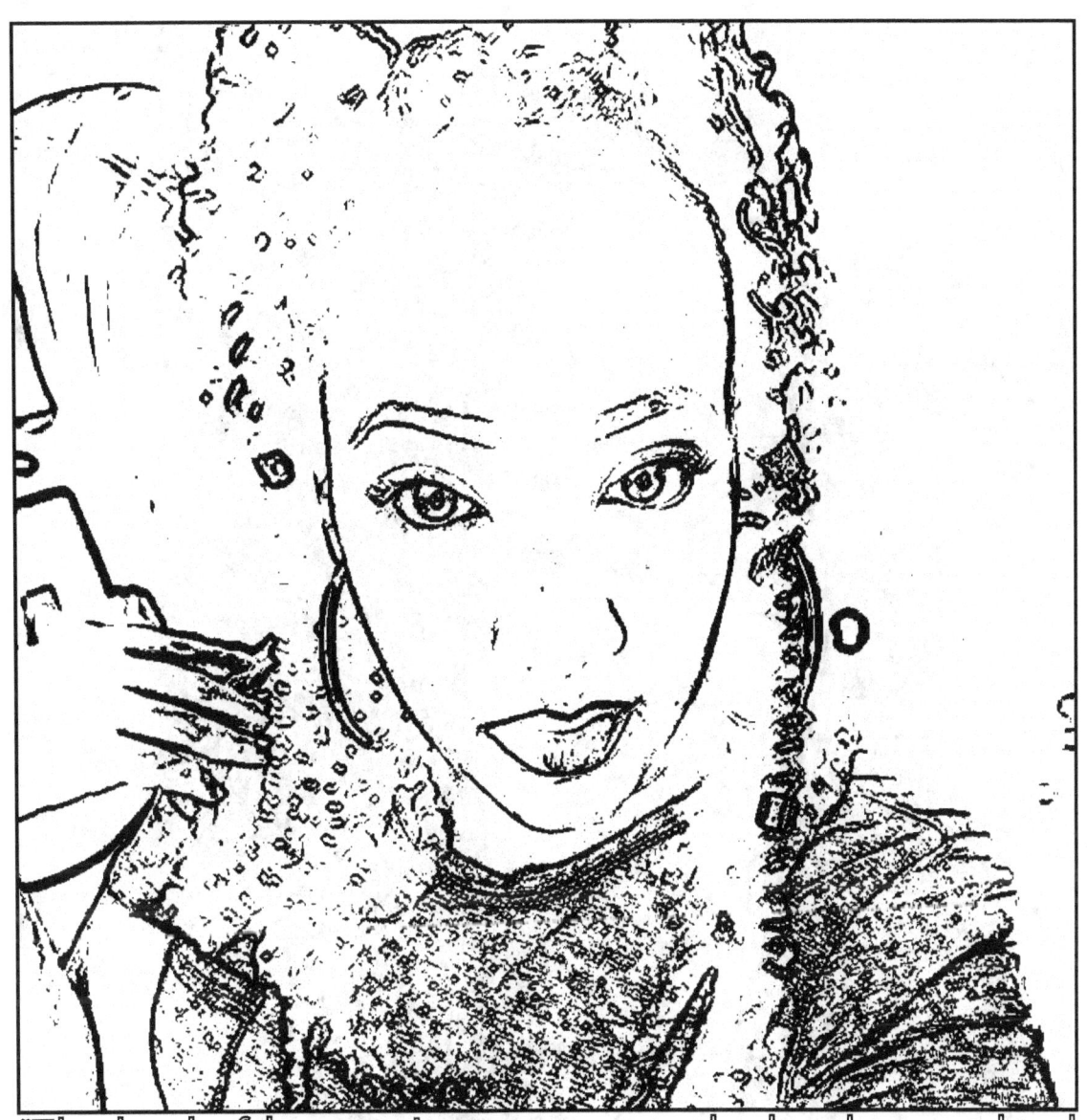

"The kind of beauty I want most is the hard-to-get kind that comes from within – strength, courage, dignity."
Ruby Dee

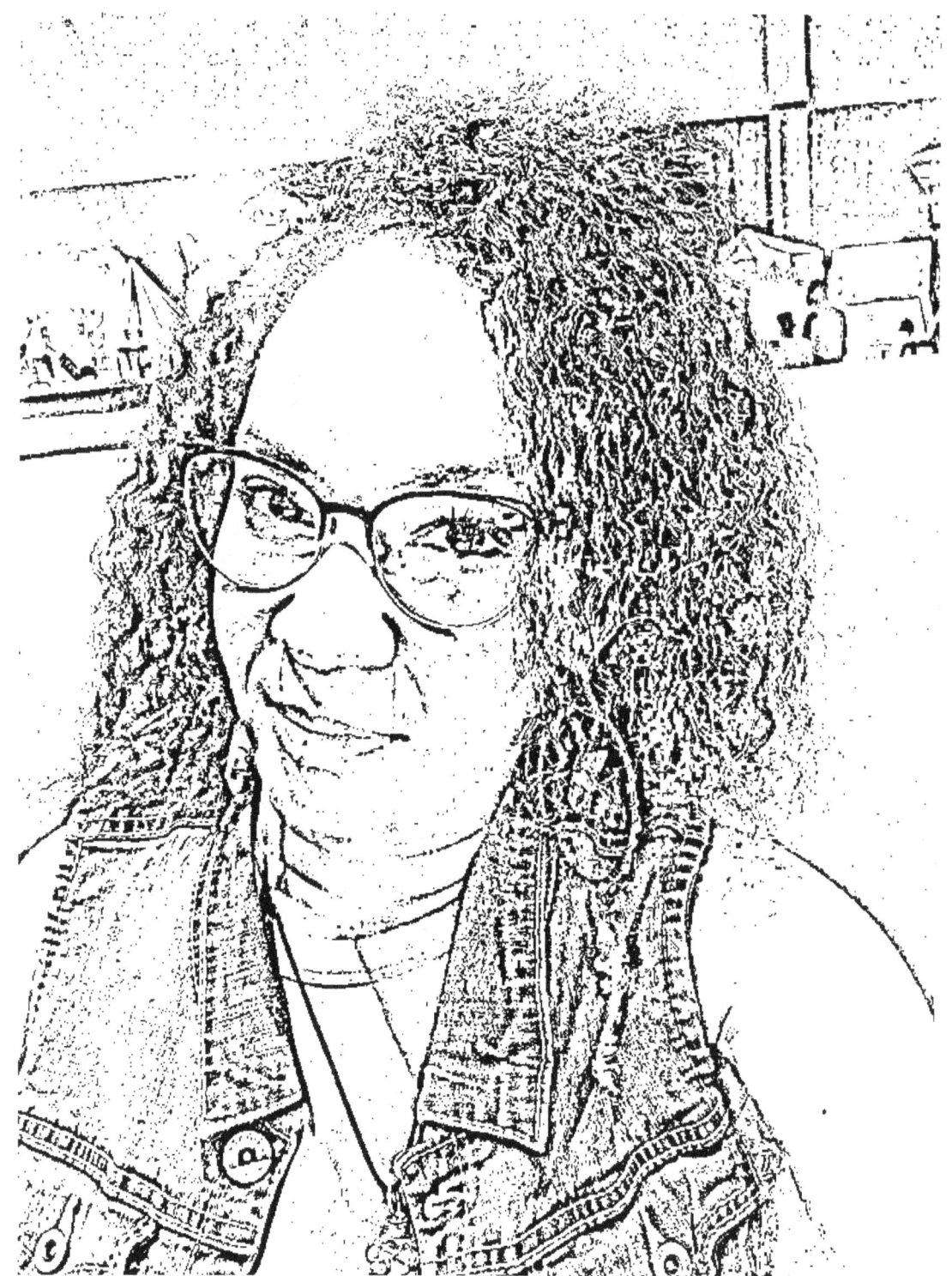

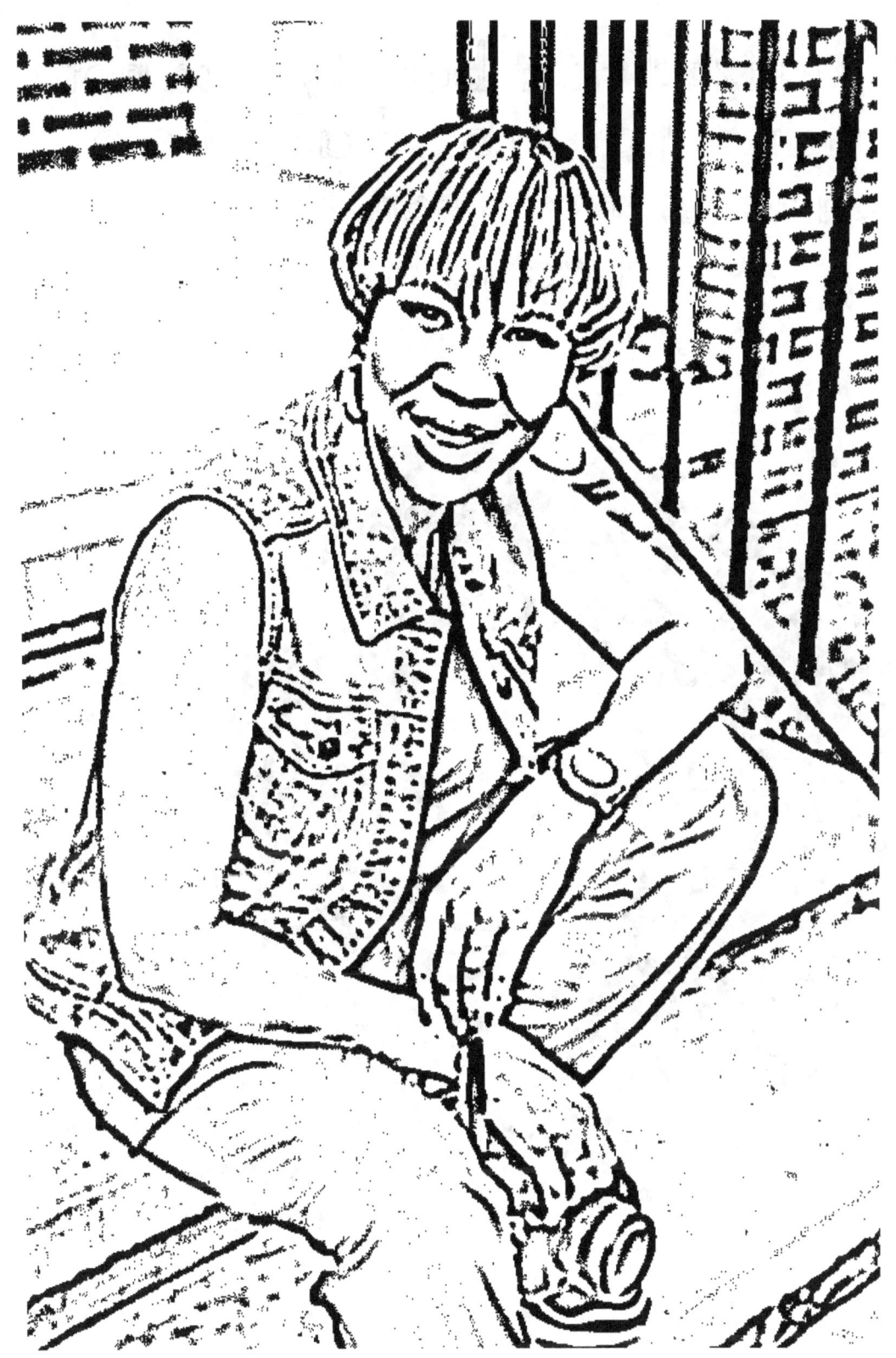

"I realized that beauty was not a thing that I could acquire or consume, it was something I just had to be."
– Lupita Nyong'o

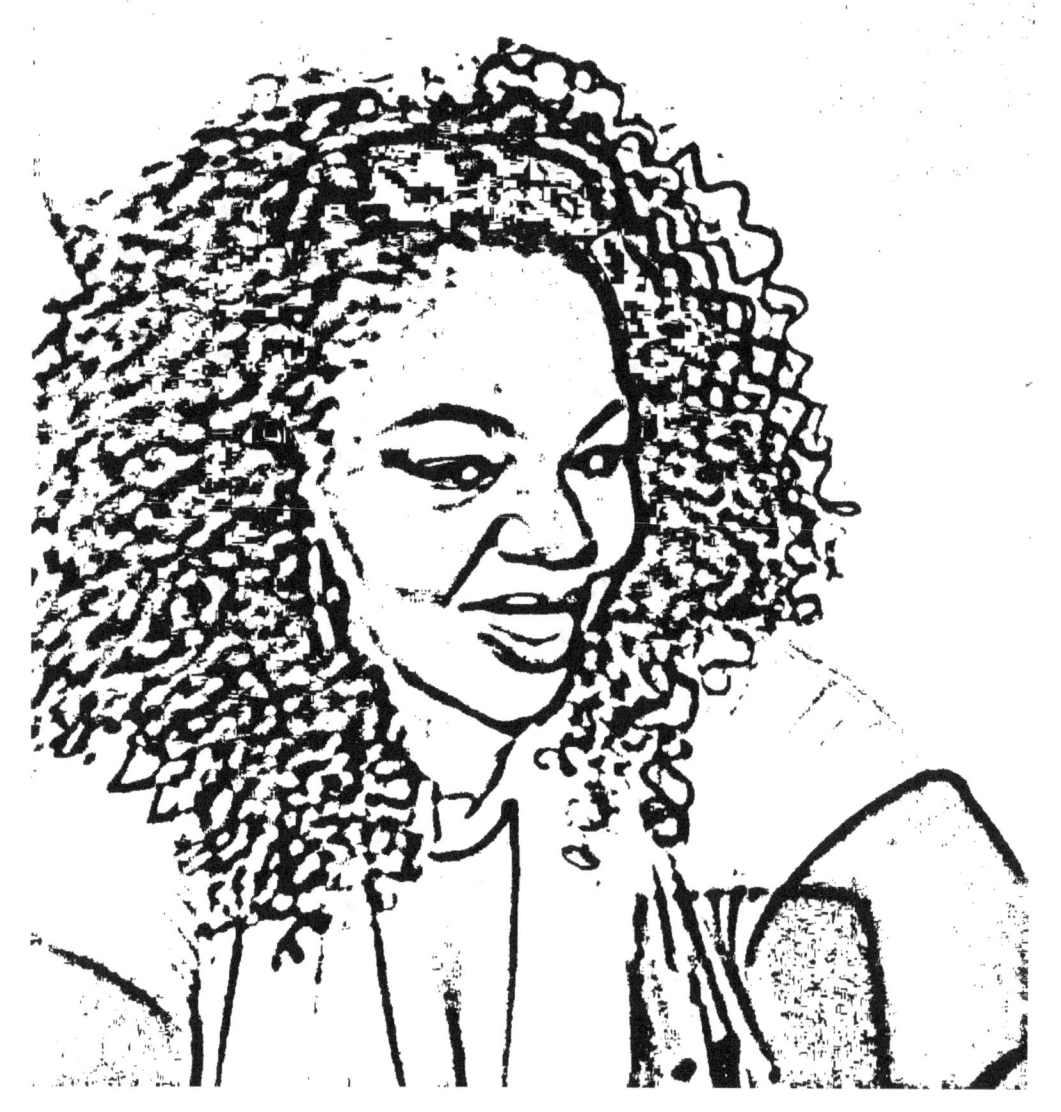

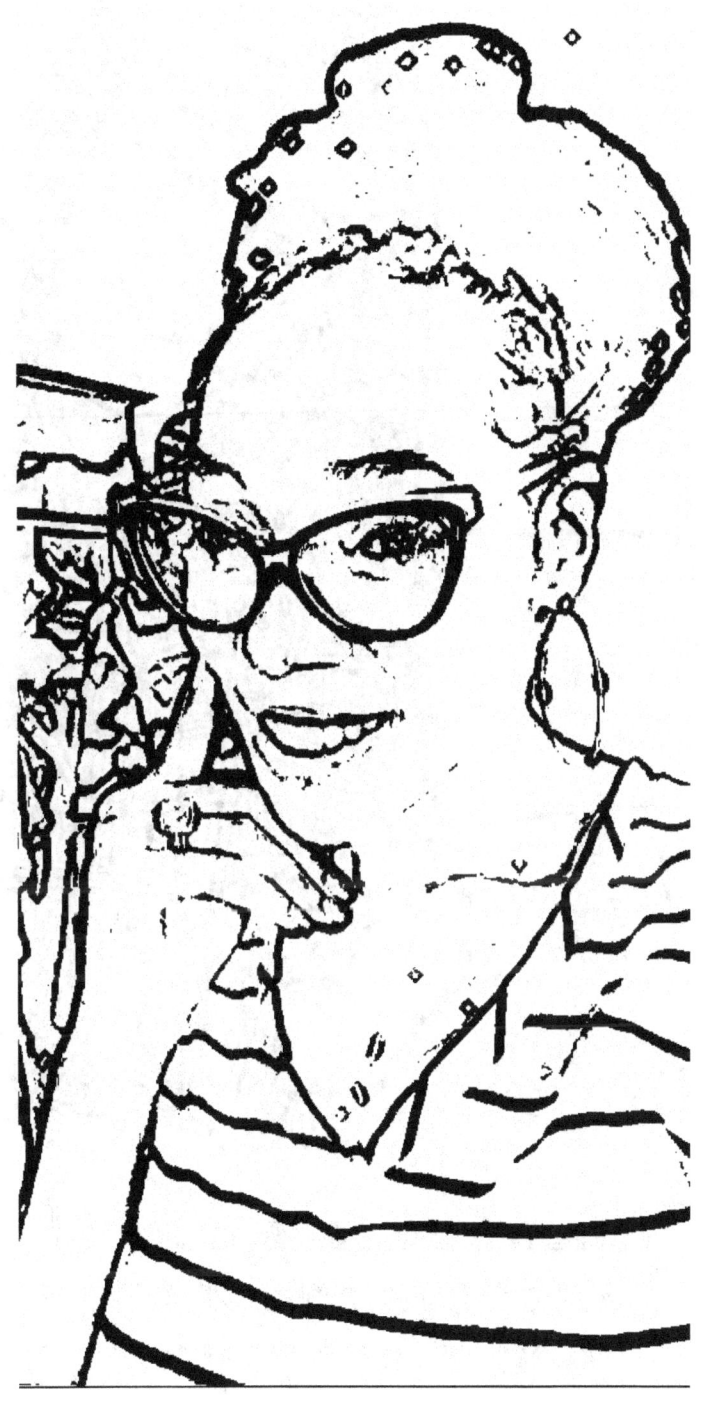

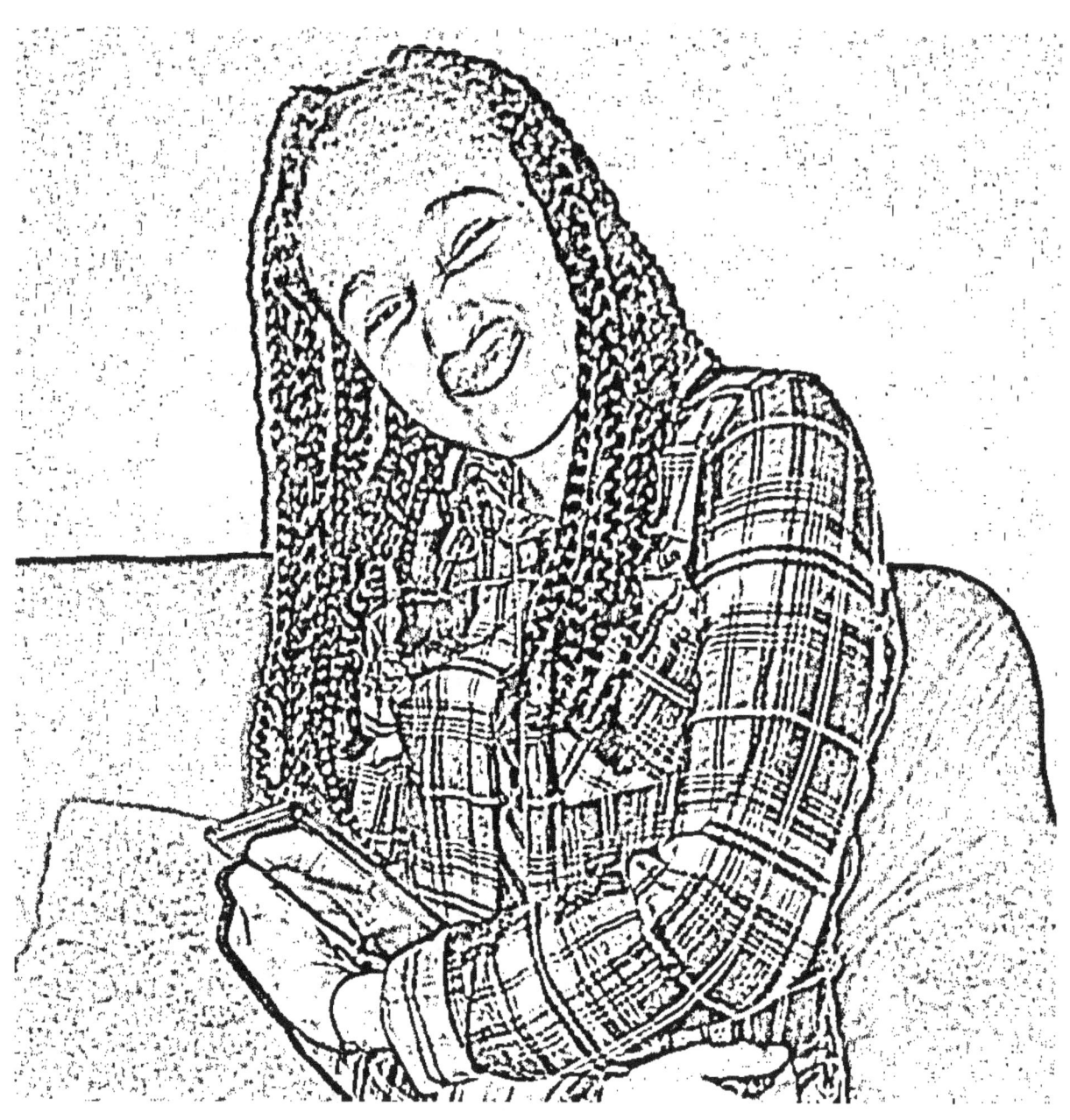

"When you take care of yourself, you're a better person for others. When you feel good about yourself, you treat others better."
– Solange

I can & I will

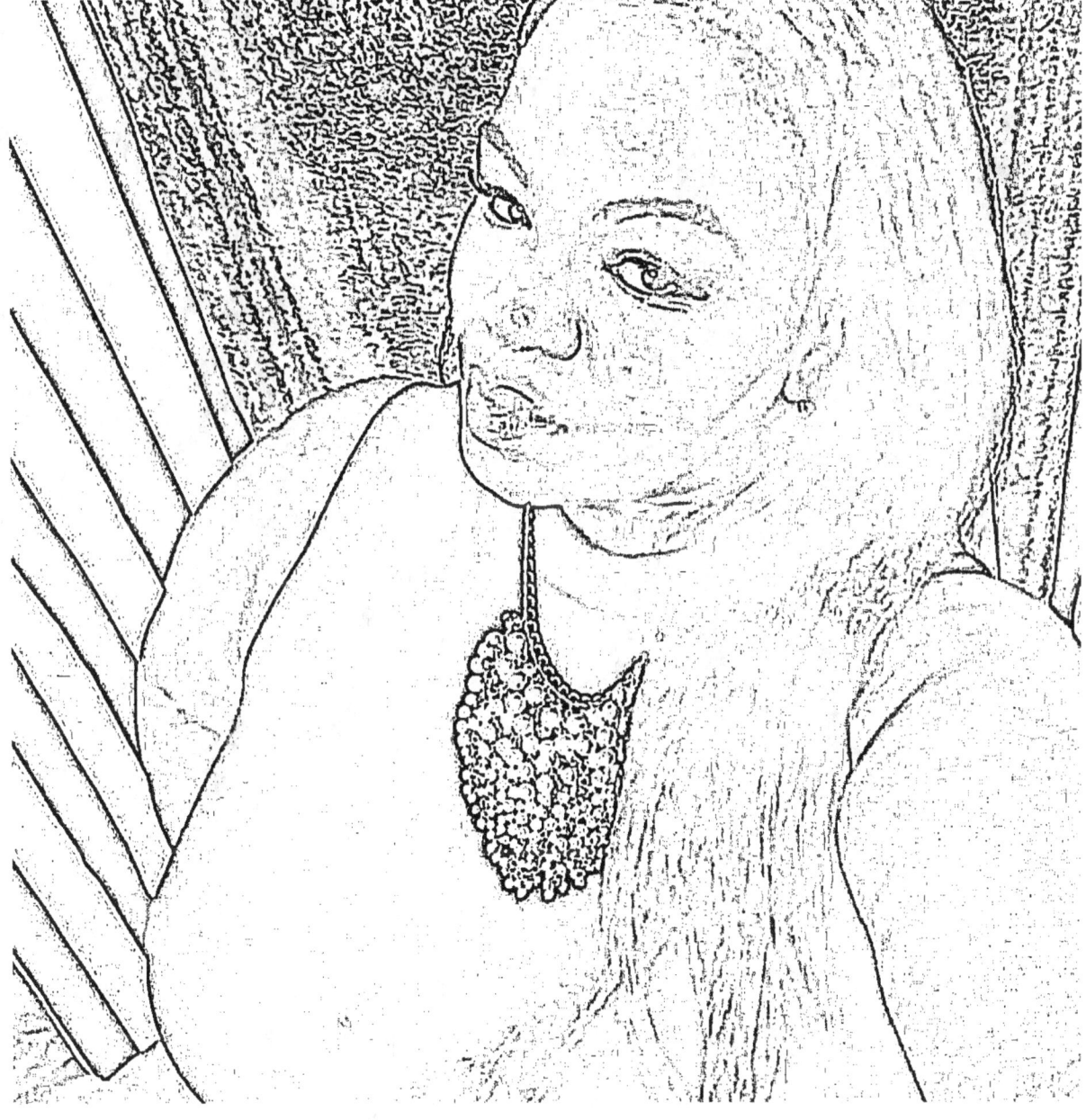

VISION

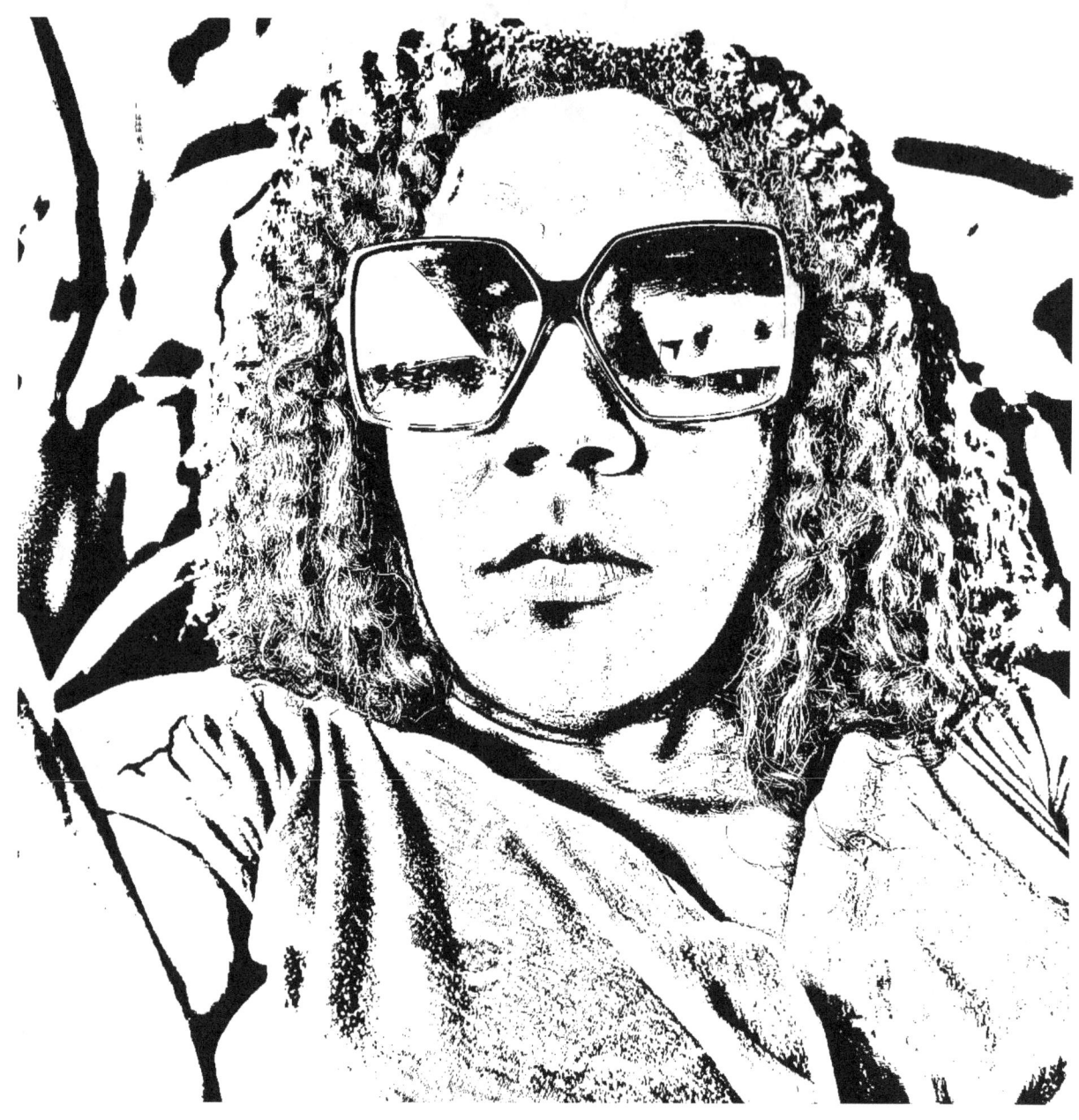

"If there's a book you really want to read, but it hasn't been written yet, then you must write it."
—Toni Morrison

"I need to see my own beauty and to continue to be reminded that I am enough, that I am worthy of love without effort, that I am beautiful, that the texture of my hair and that the shape of my curves, the size of my lips, the color of my skin, and the feelings that I have are all worthy and okay." -Tracee Ellis Ross

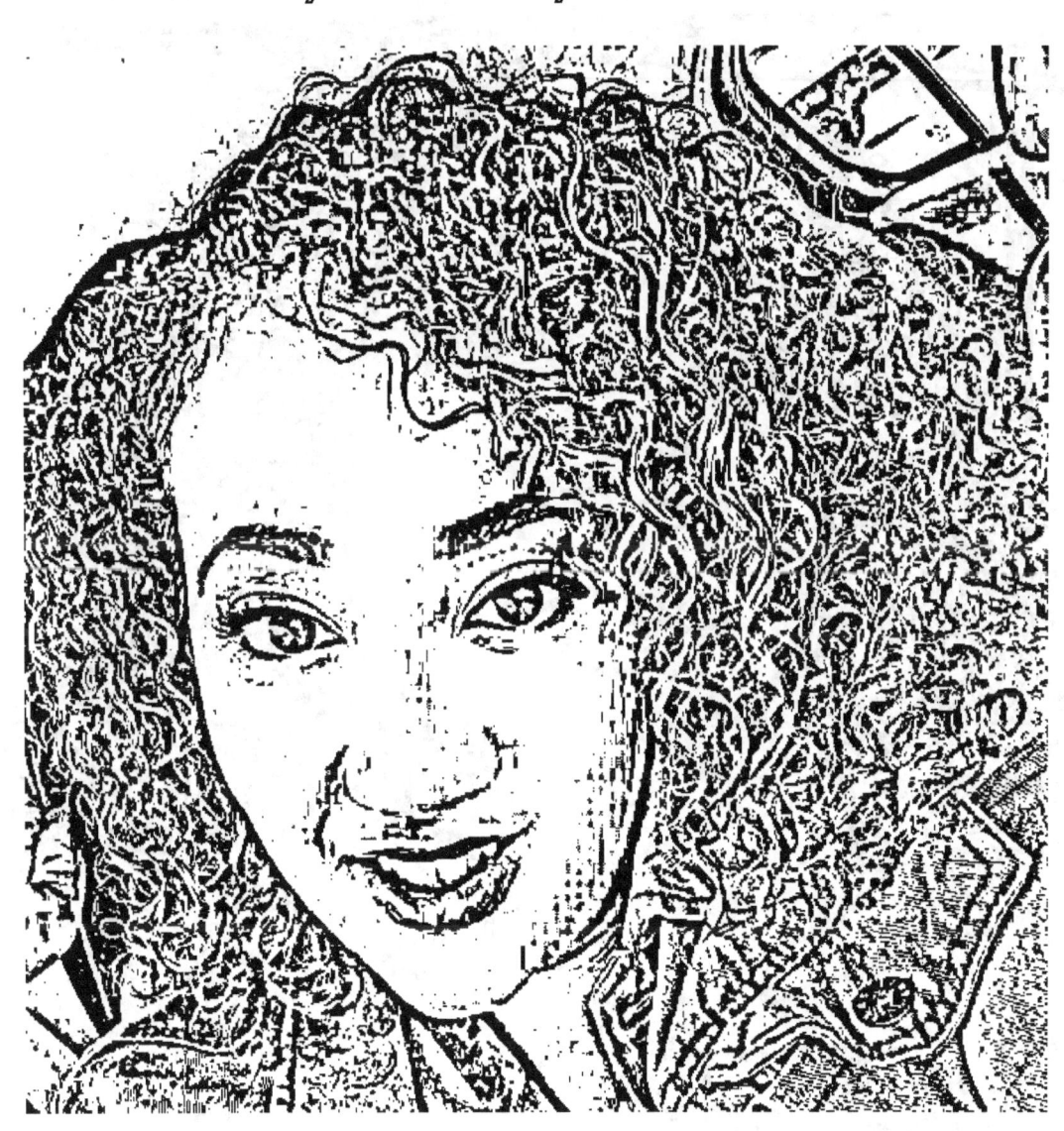

"Never give up, for that is just the place and time that the tide will turn."
- Harriet Beecher Stowe

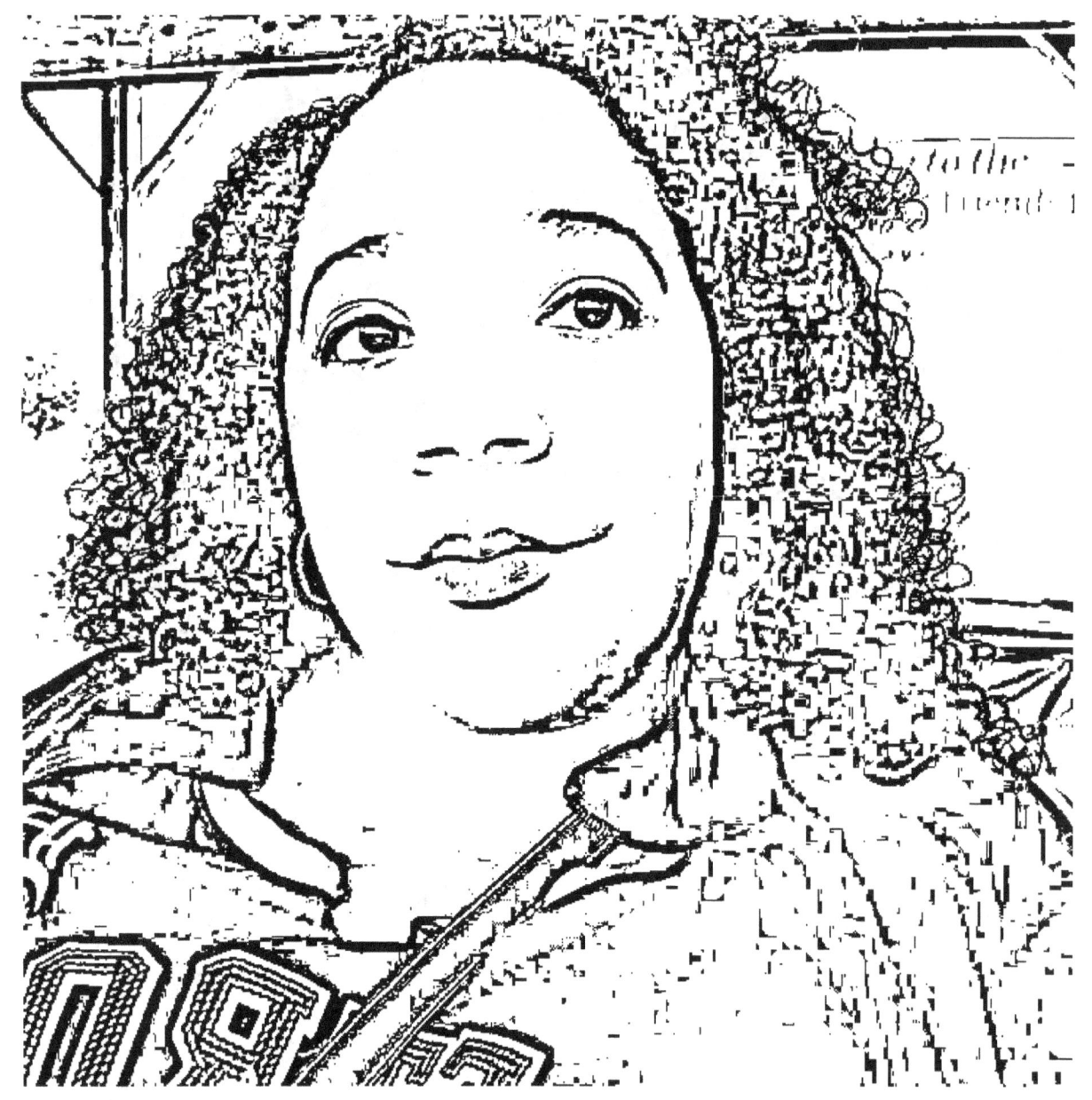

BE BRAVE

SHINE BRIGHT

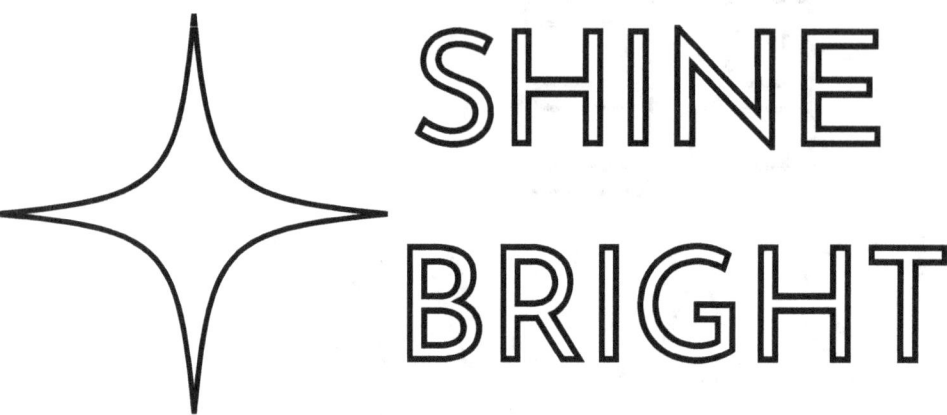

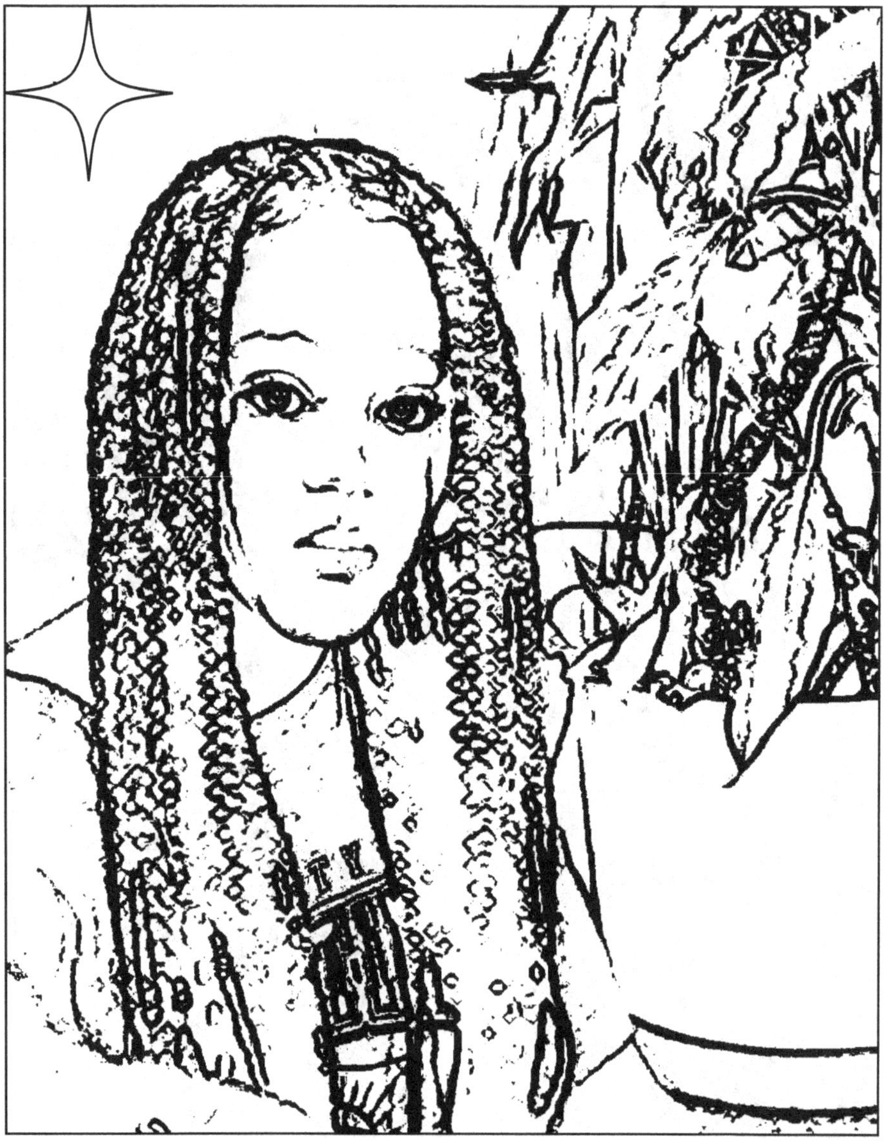

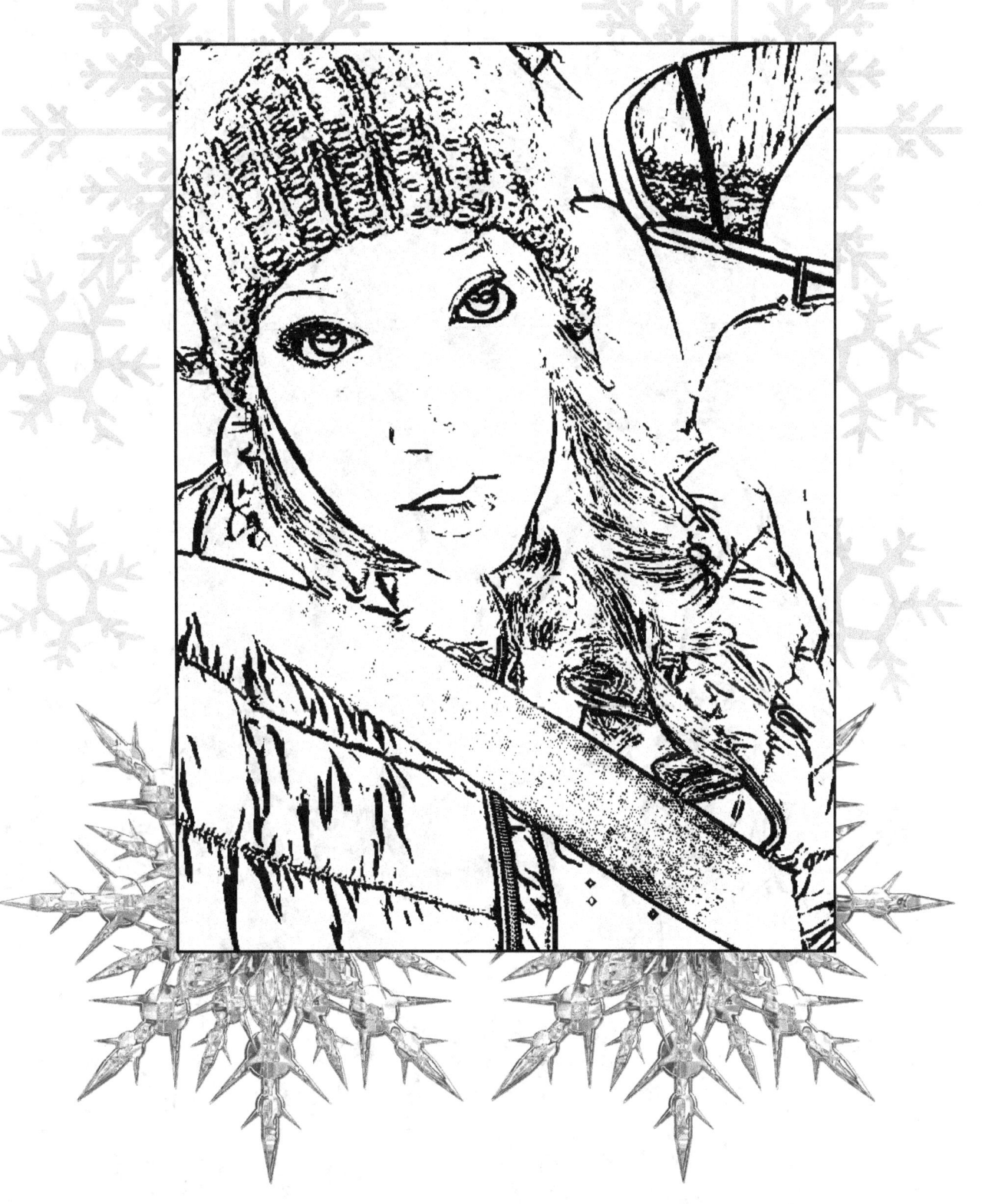

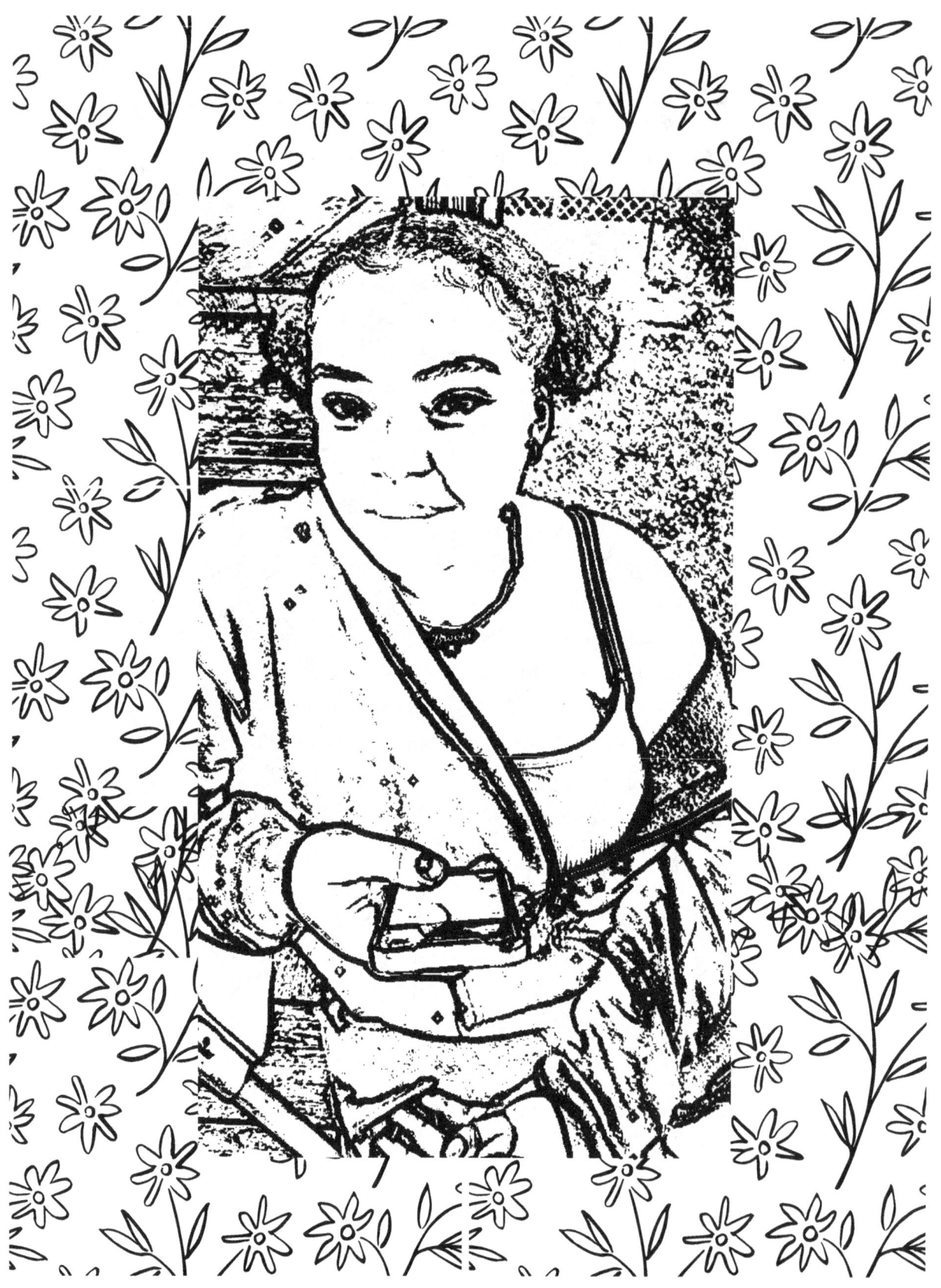

"I got my start by giving myself a start." – Madame CJ Walker

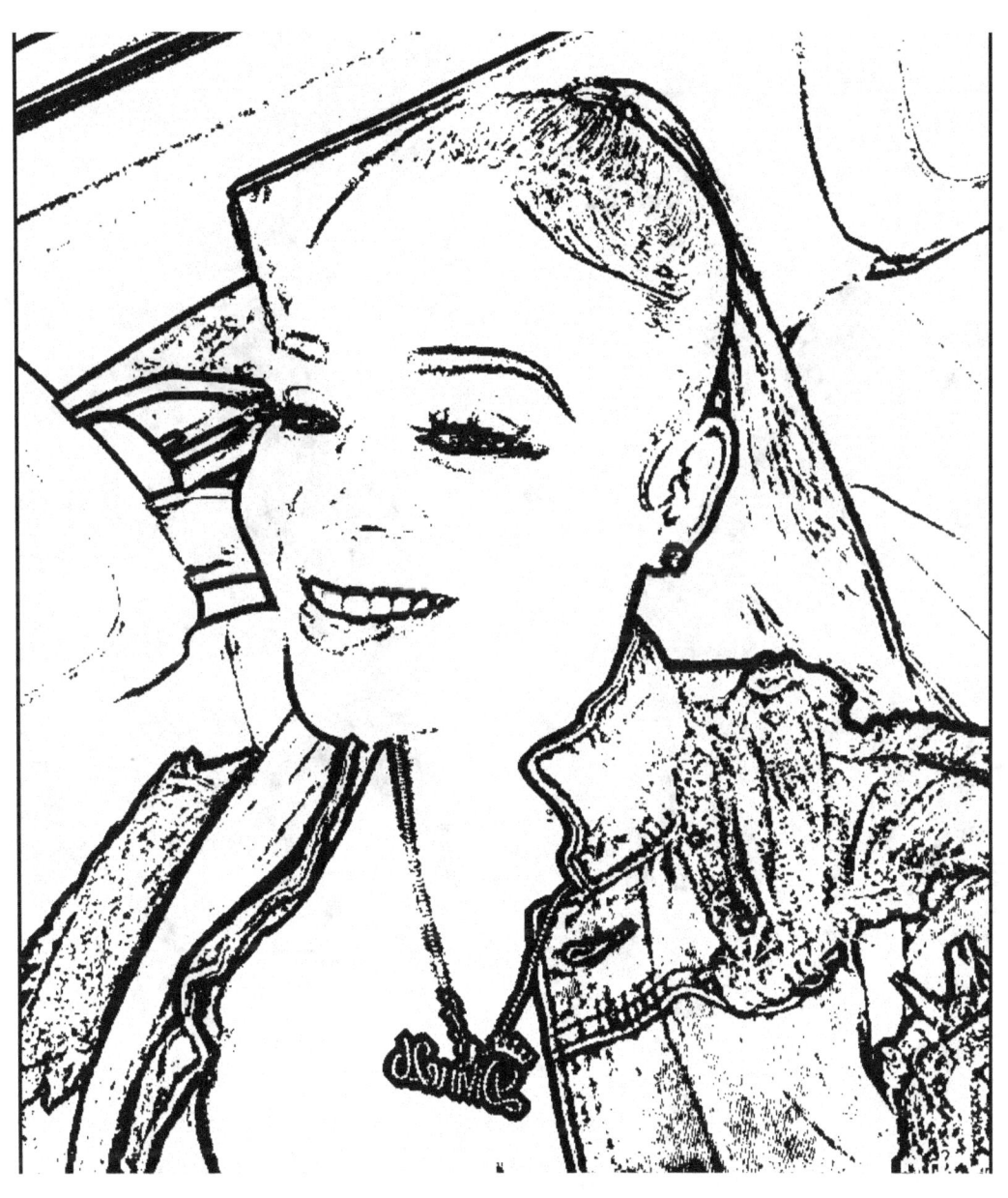

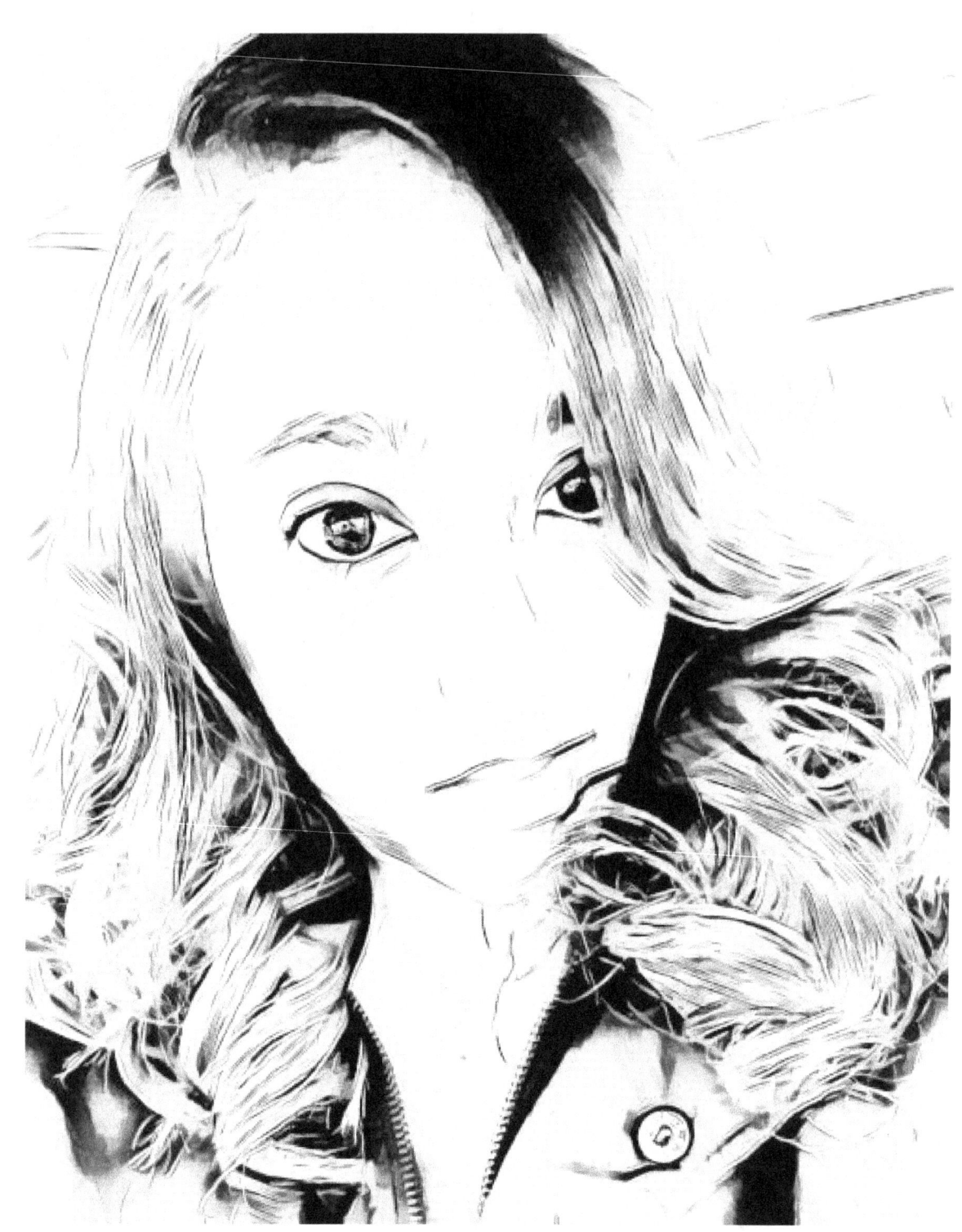

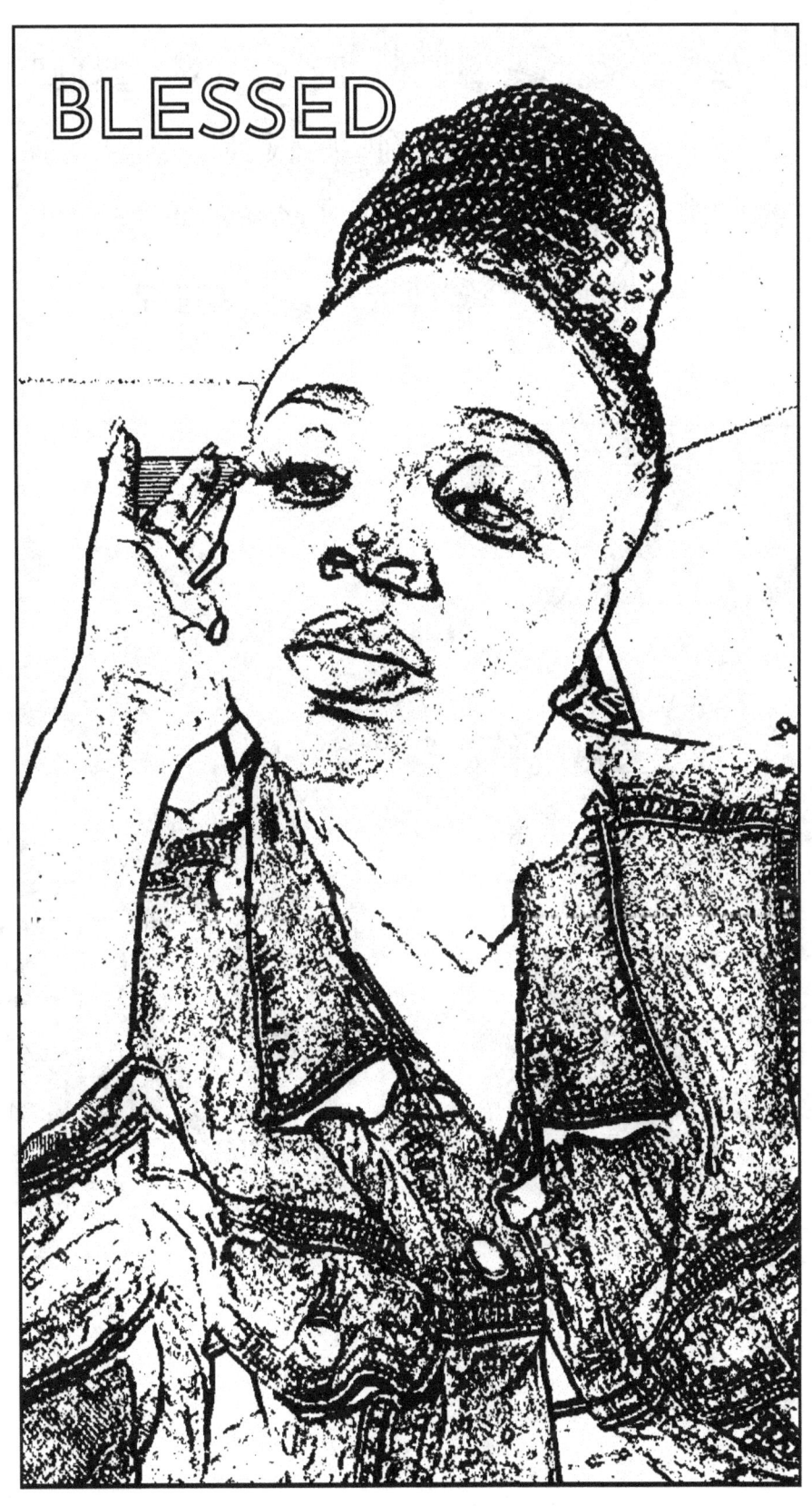

"There are still many causes worth sacrificing for, so much history yet to be made."
—Michelle Obama

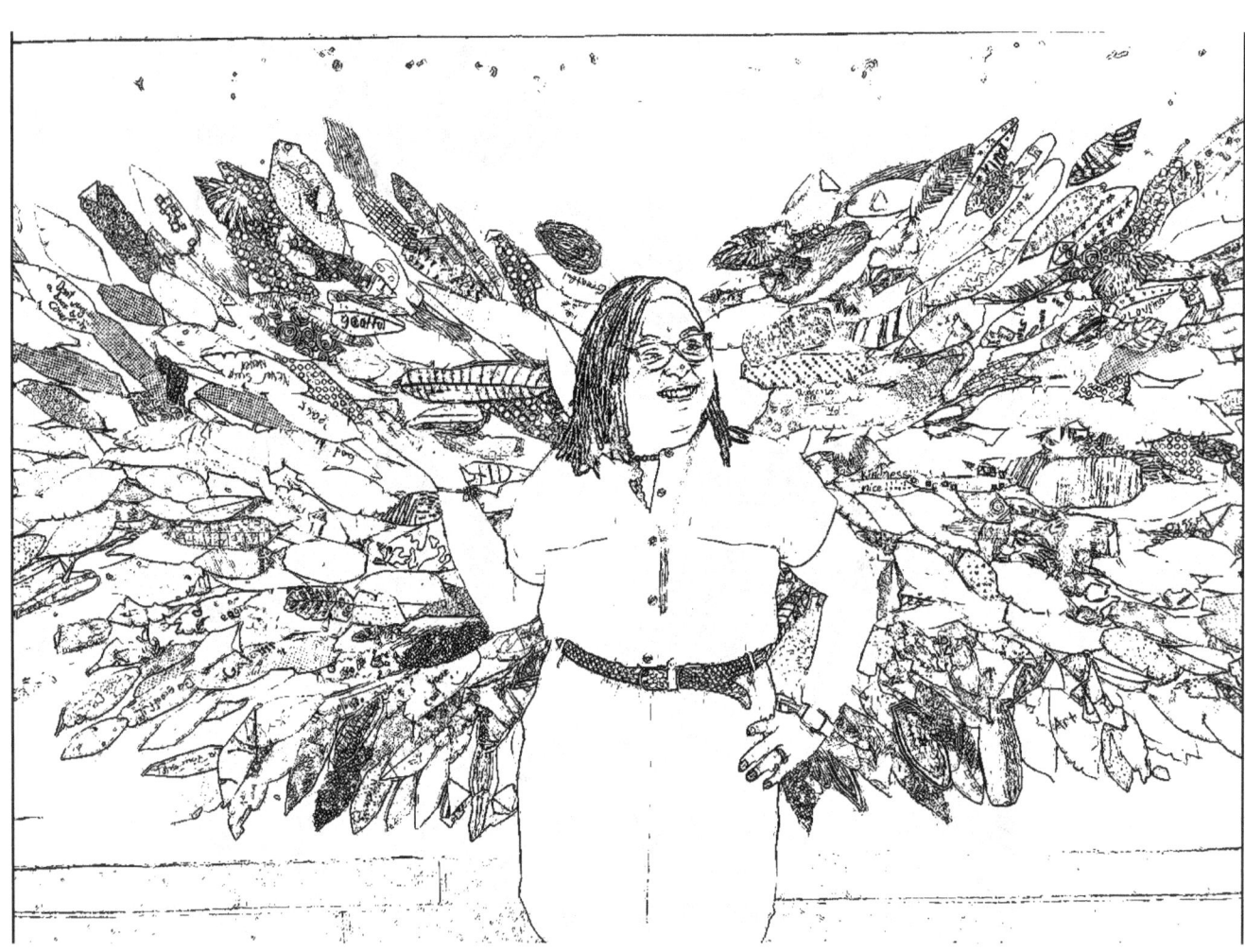

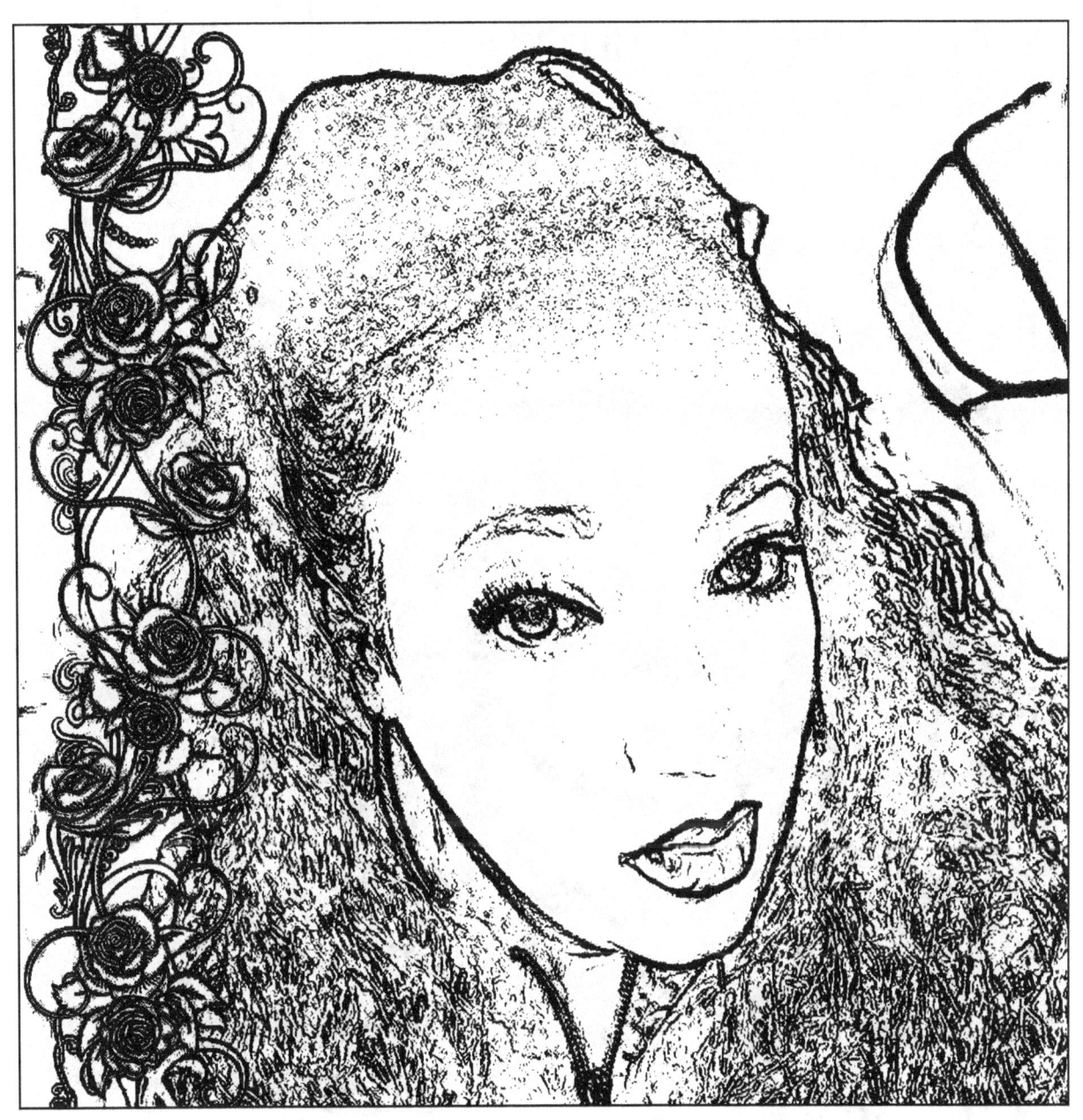

"You have the power to change perception, to inspire and empower, and to show people how to embrace their complications, and see the flaws, and the true beauty and strength that's inside all of us."
— Beyoncé

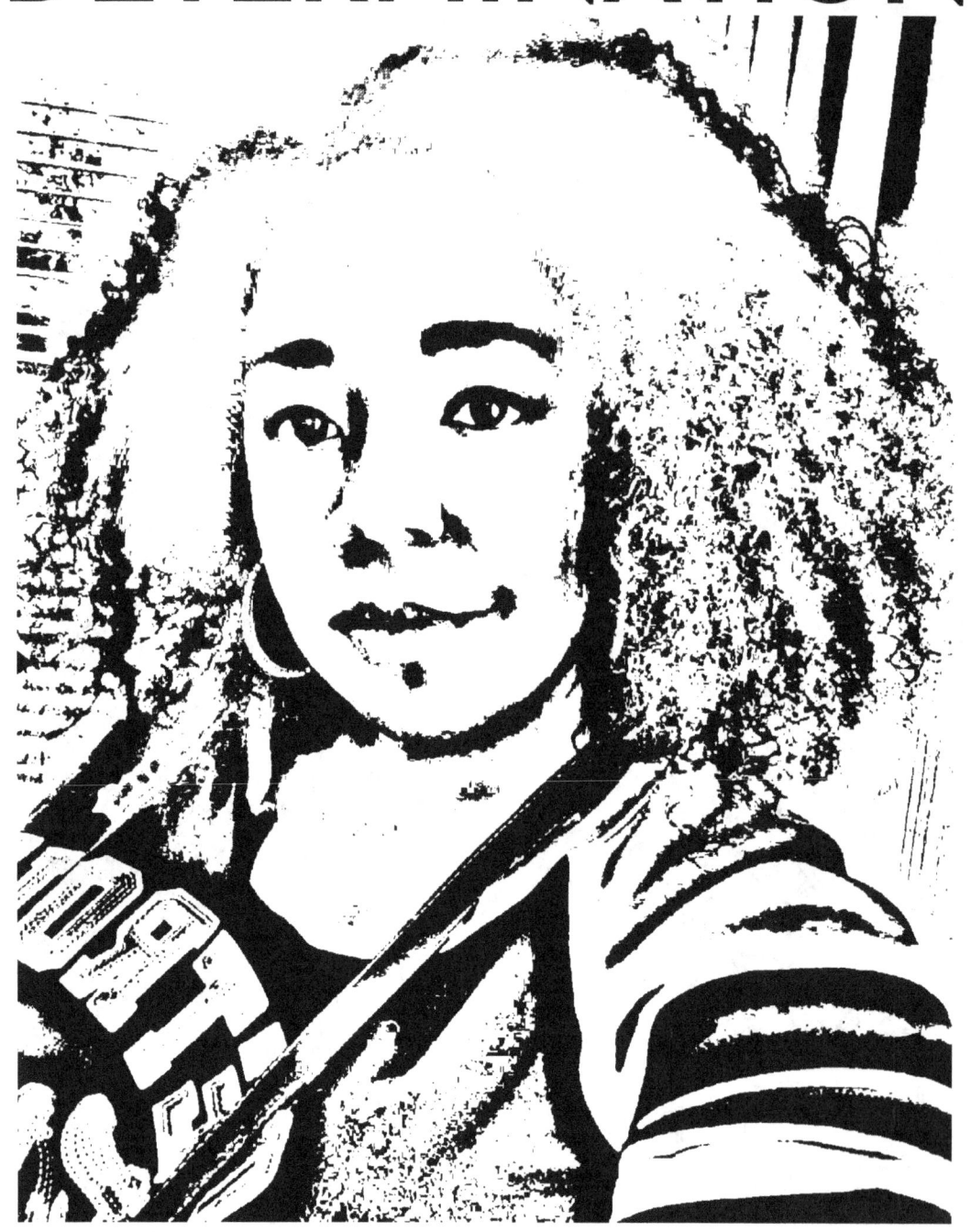

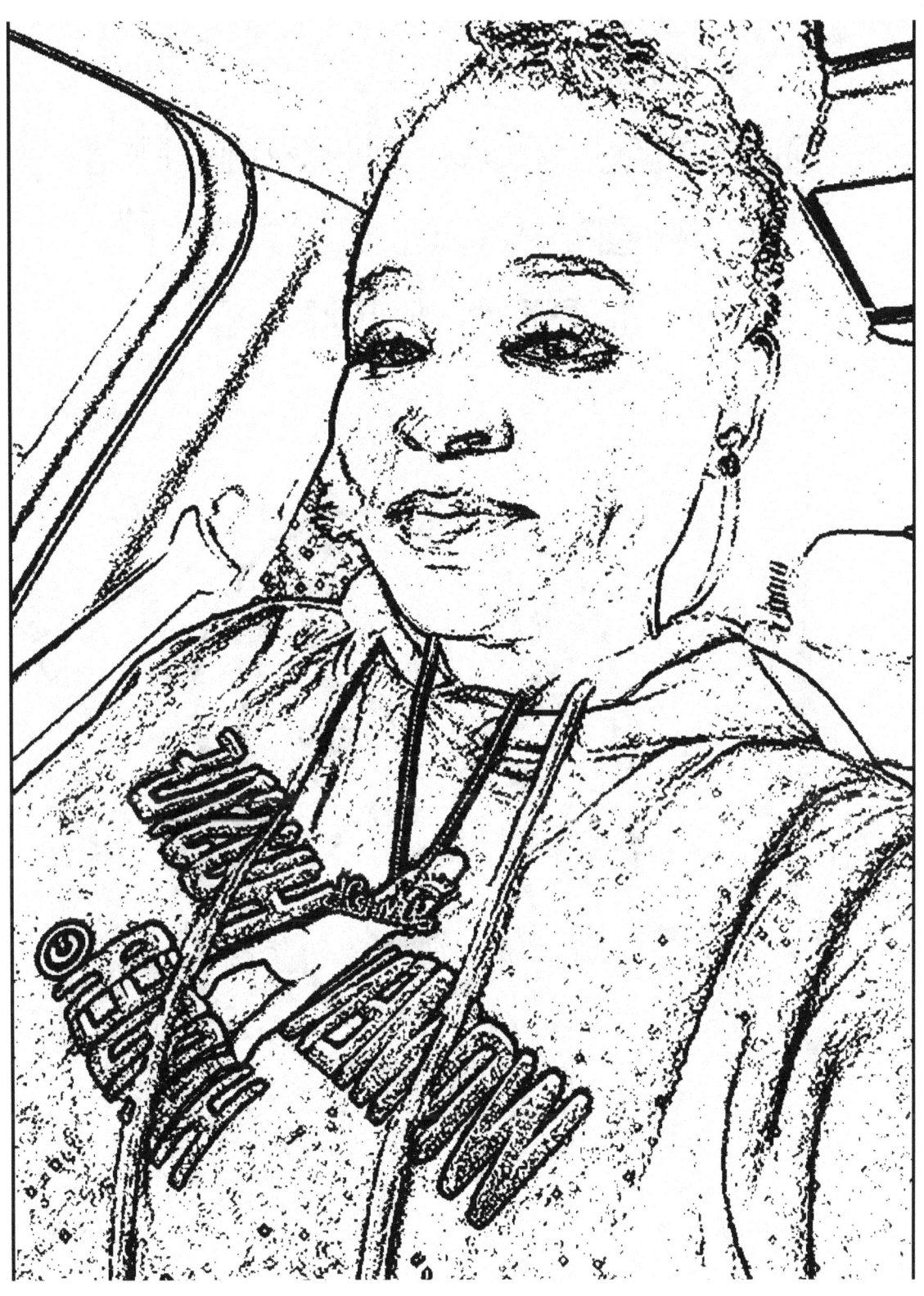

"It's not the load that breaks you down, it's the way you carry it."
- Lena Horne

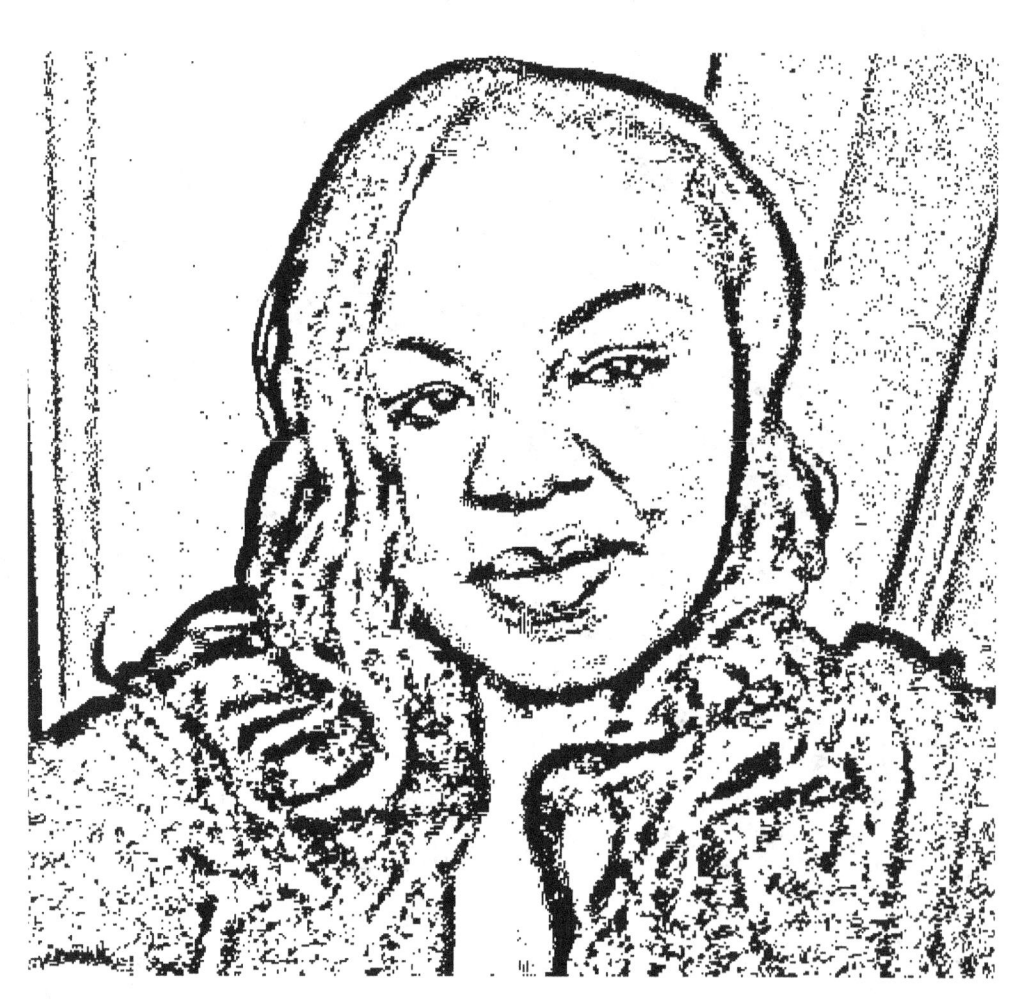

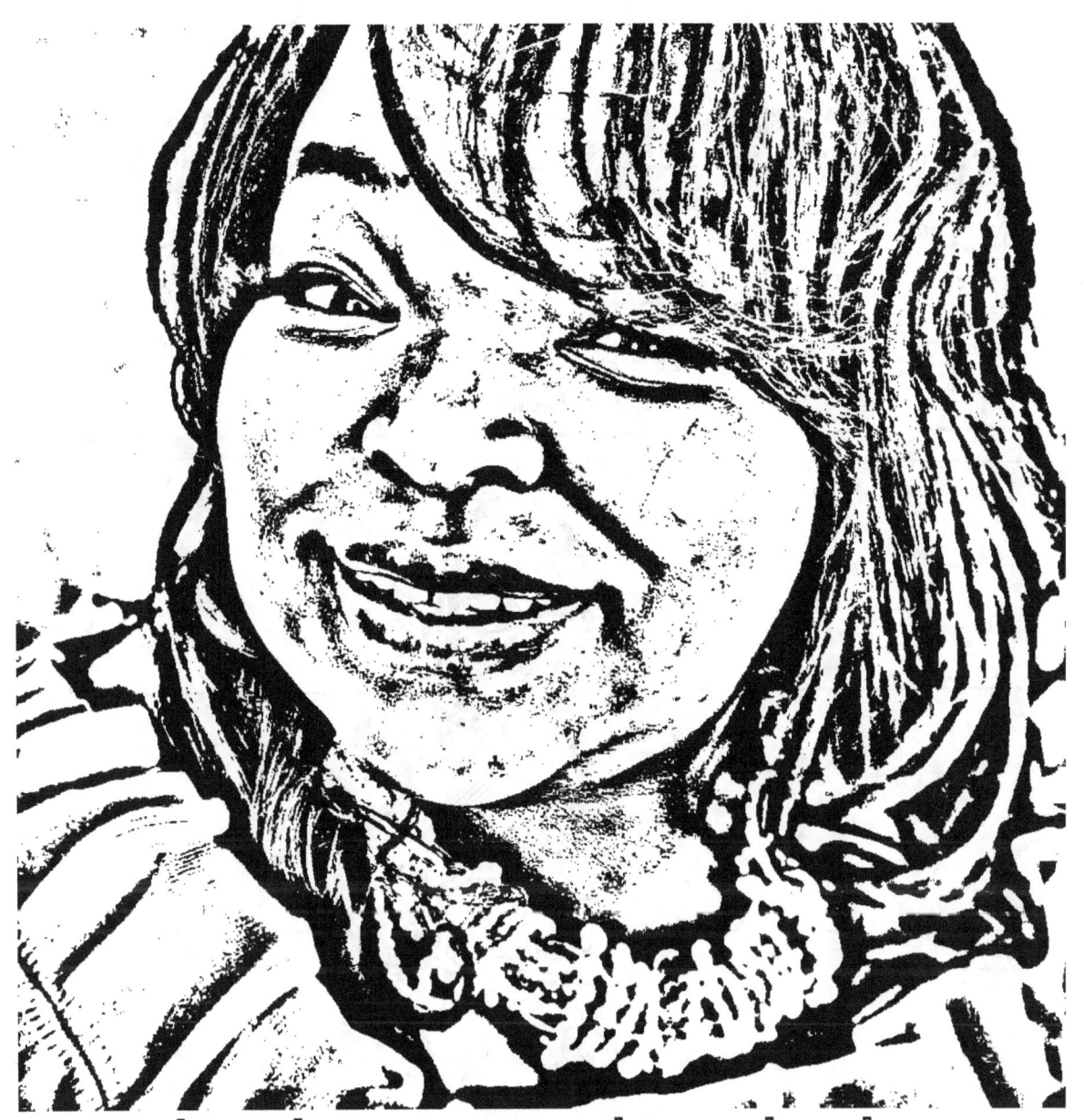

"I'd rather regret the risks that didn't work out than the chances I didn't take at all."
- Simone Biles

"Success doesn't come to you...
you go to it."
- Marva Collins

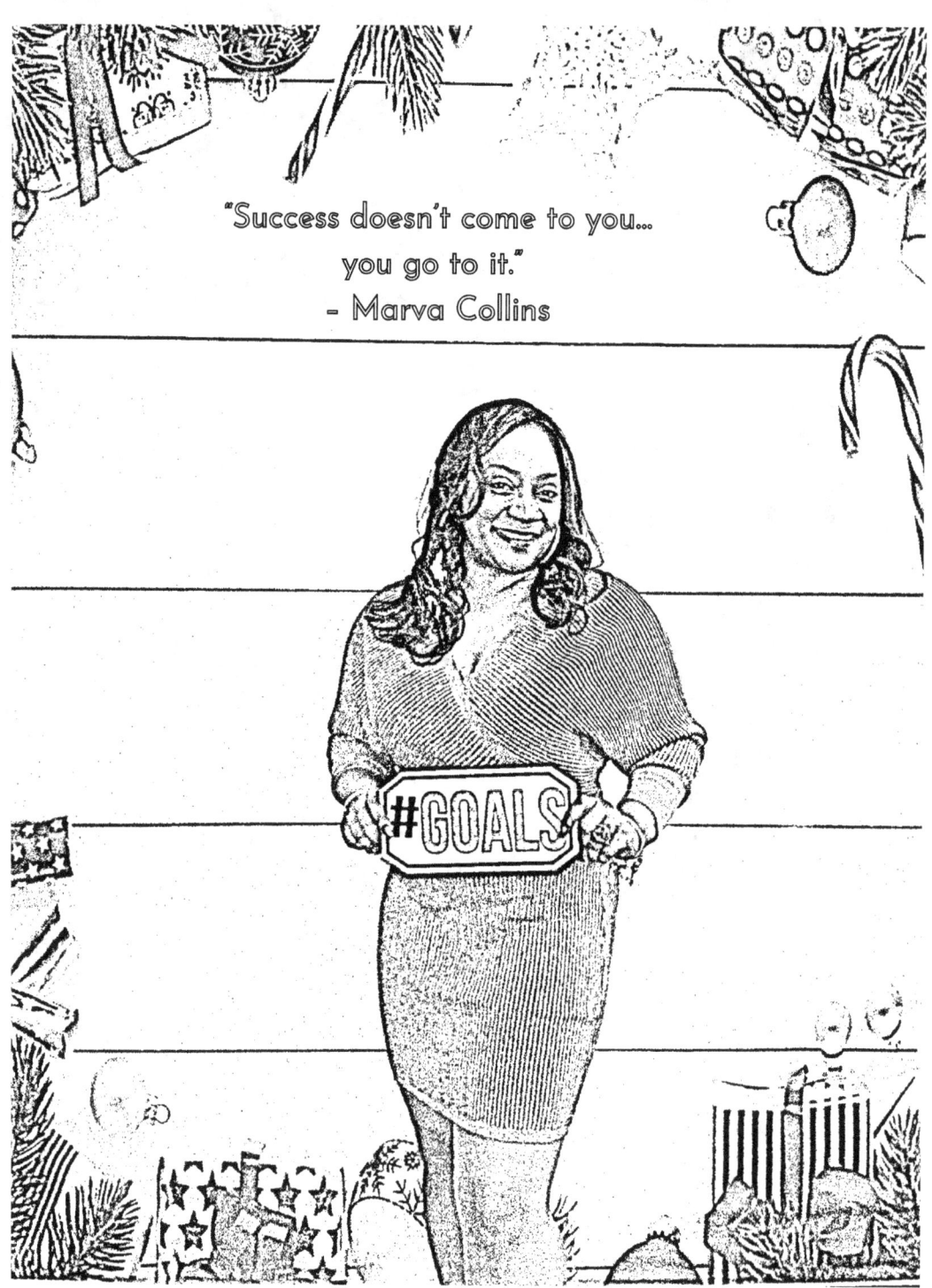

"You can fall, but you can rise also." - Angelique Kidjo

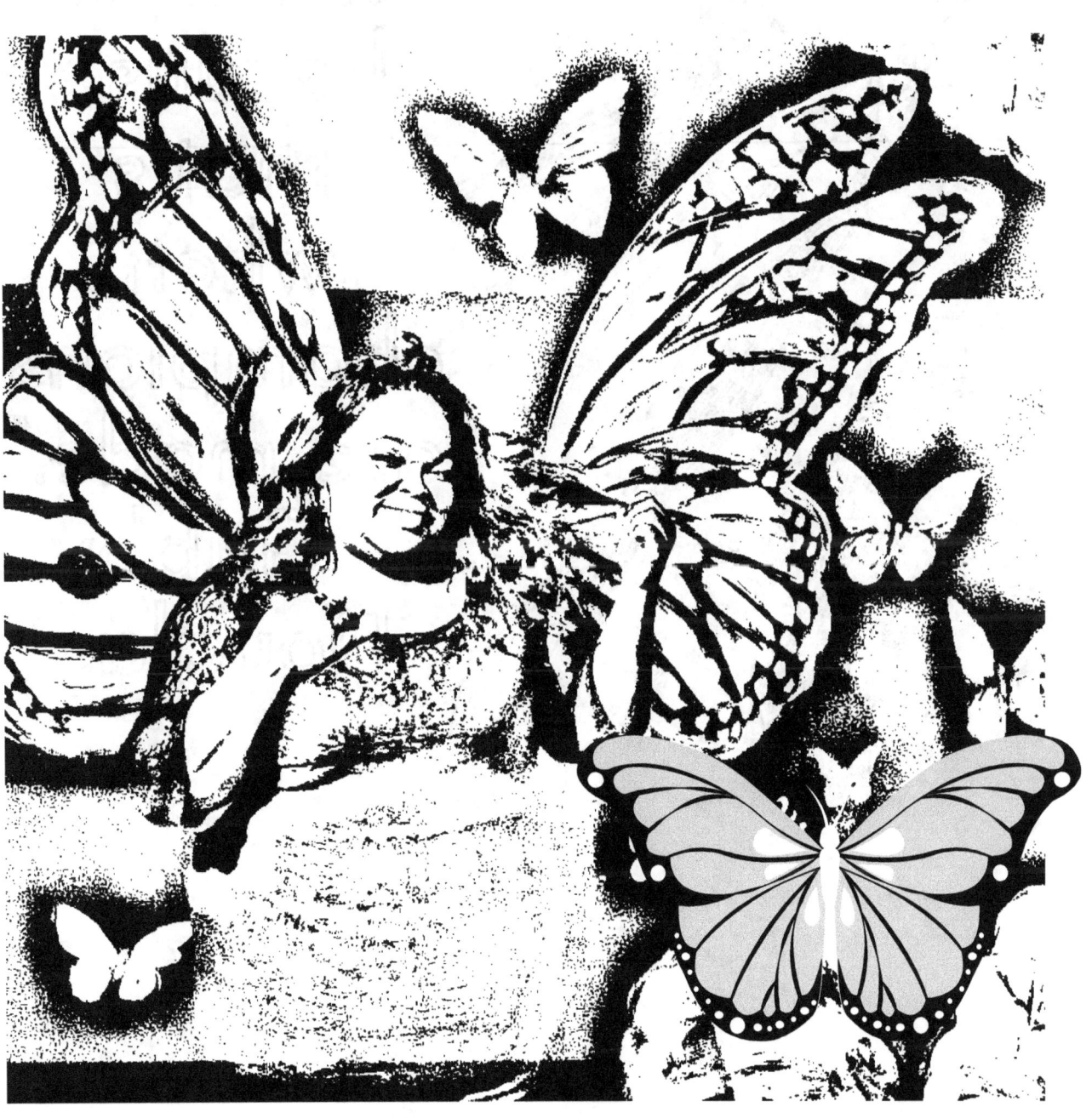

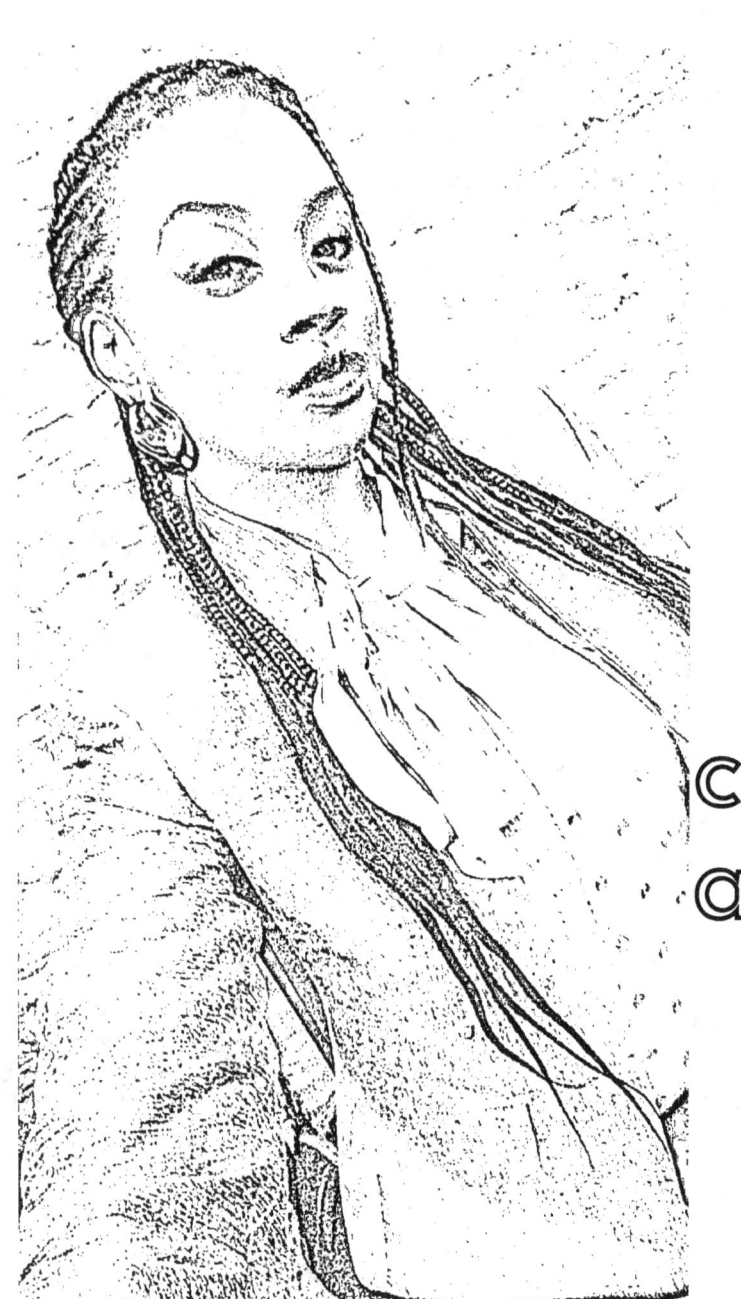

"Hard days are the best because that's when champions are made."
- Gabby Douglas

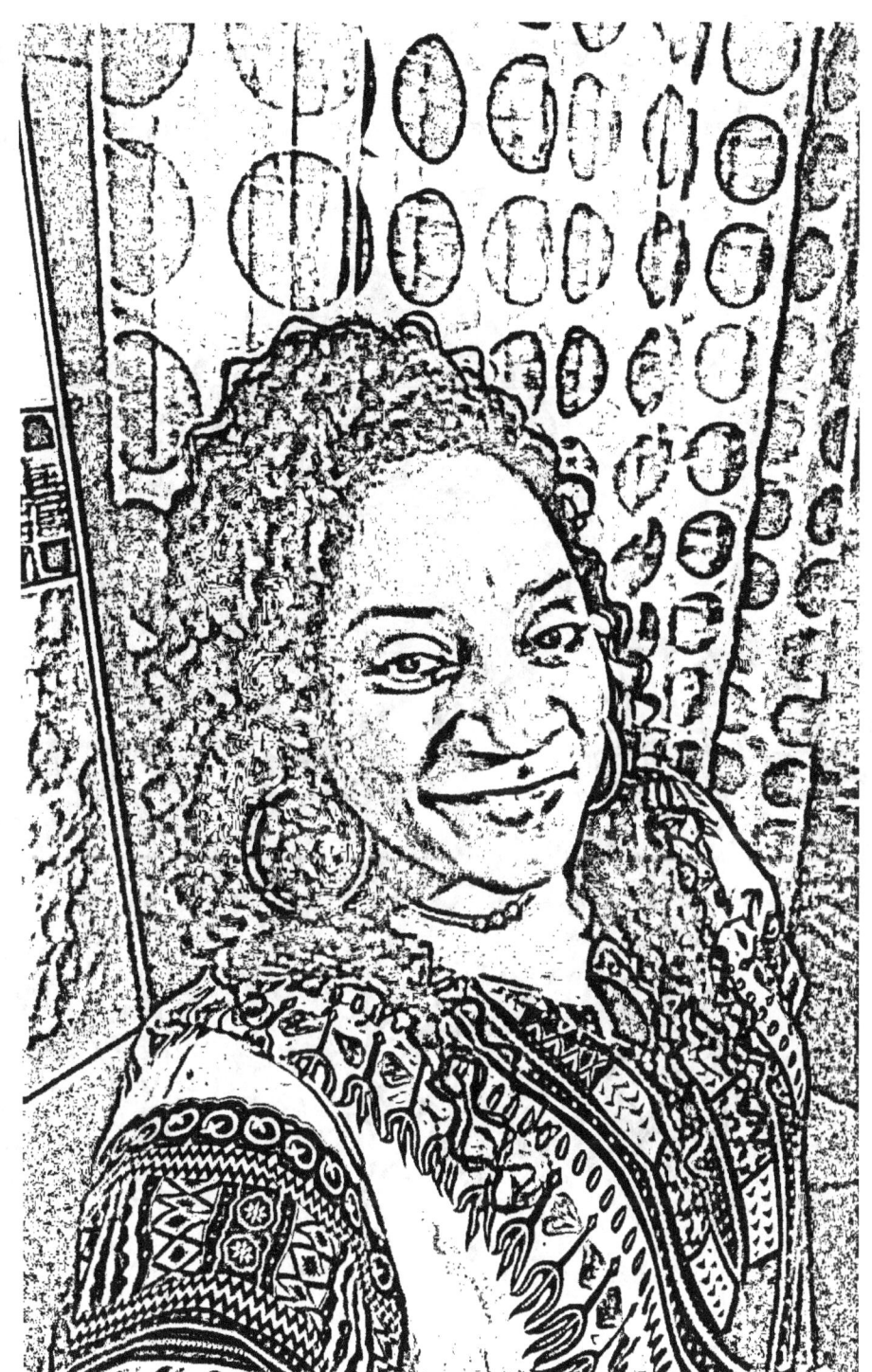

"Be passionate and move forward with gusto every single hour of every single day until you reach your goal."
— Ava DuVernay

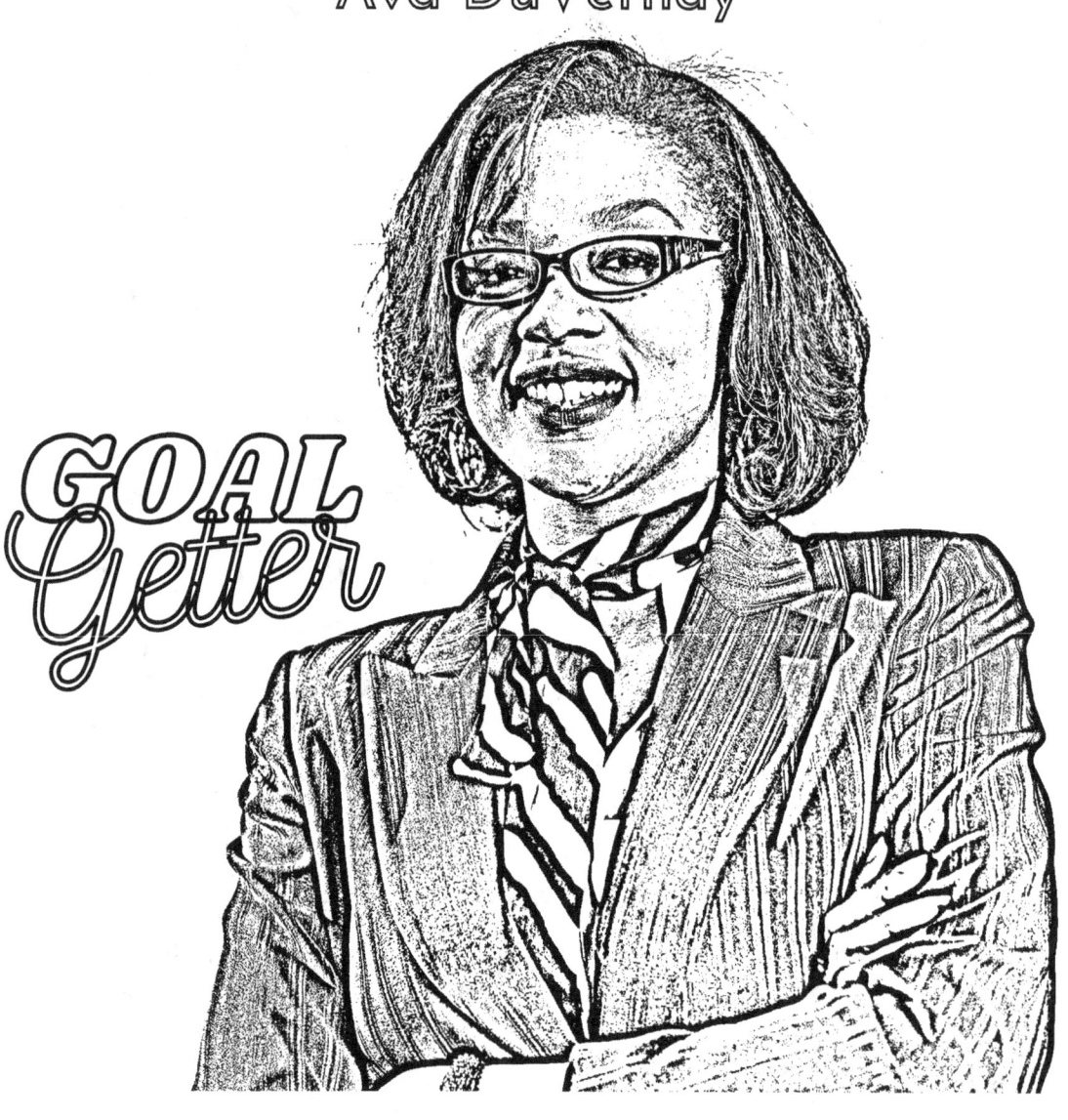

"I have learned over the years that when one's mind is made up, this diminishes fear; knowing what must be done does away with fear."
- Rosa Parks

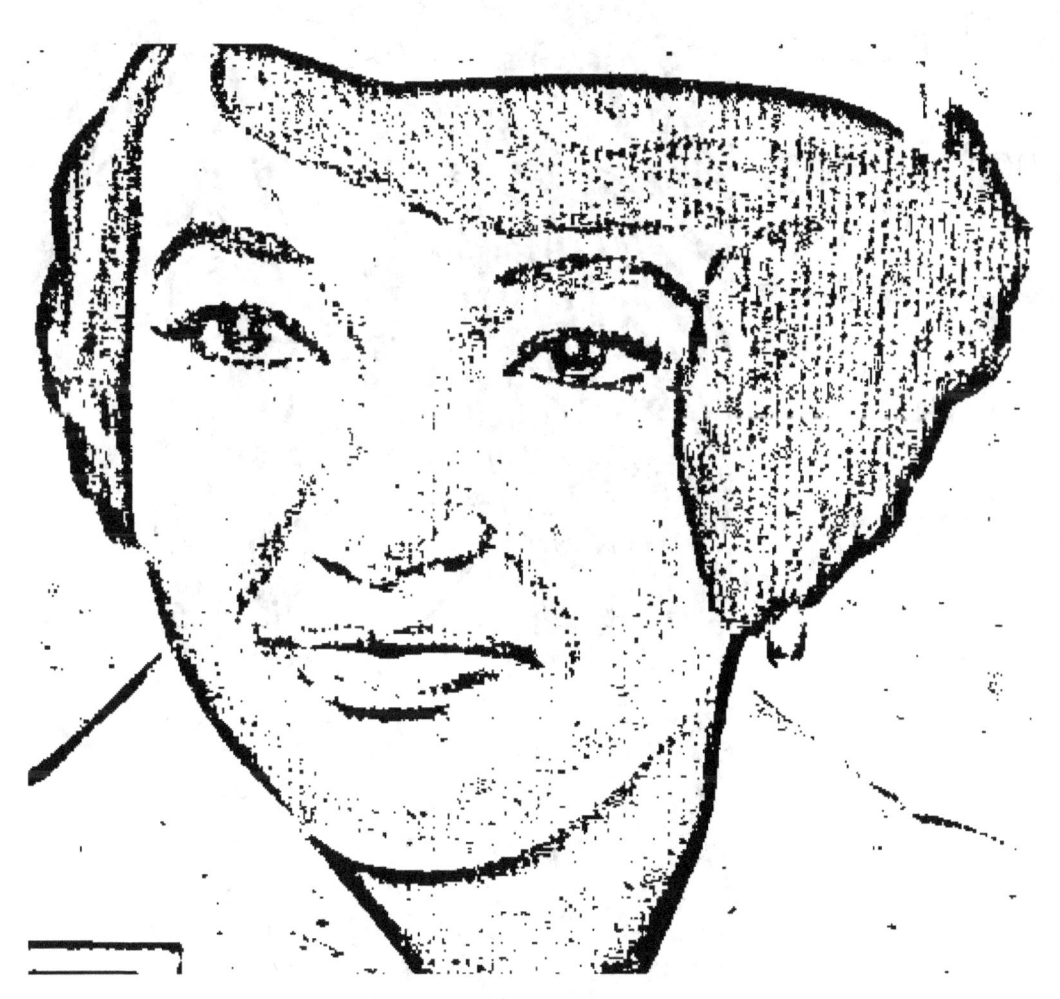

"Magic lies in challenging what seems impossible." - Carol Moseley Braun

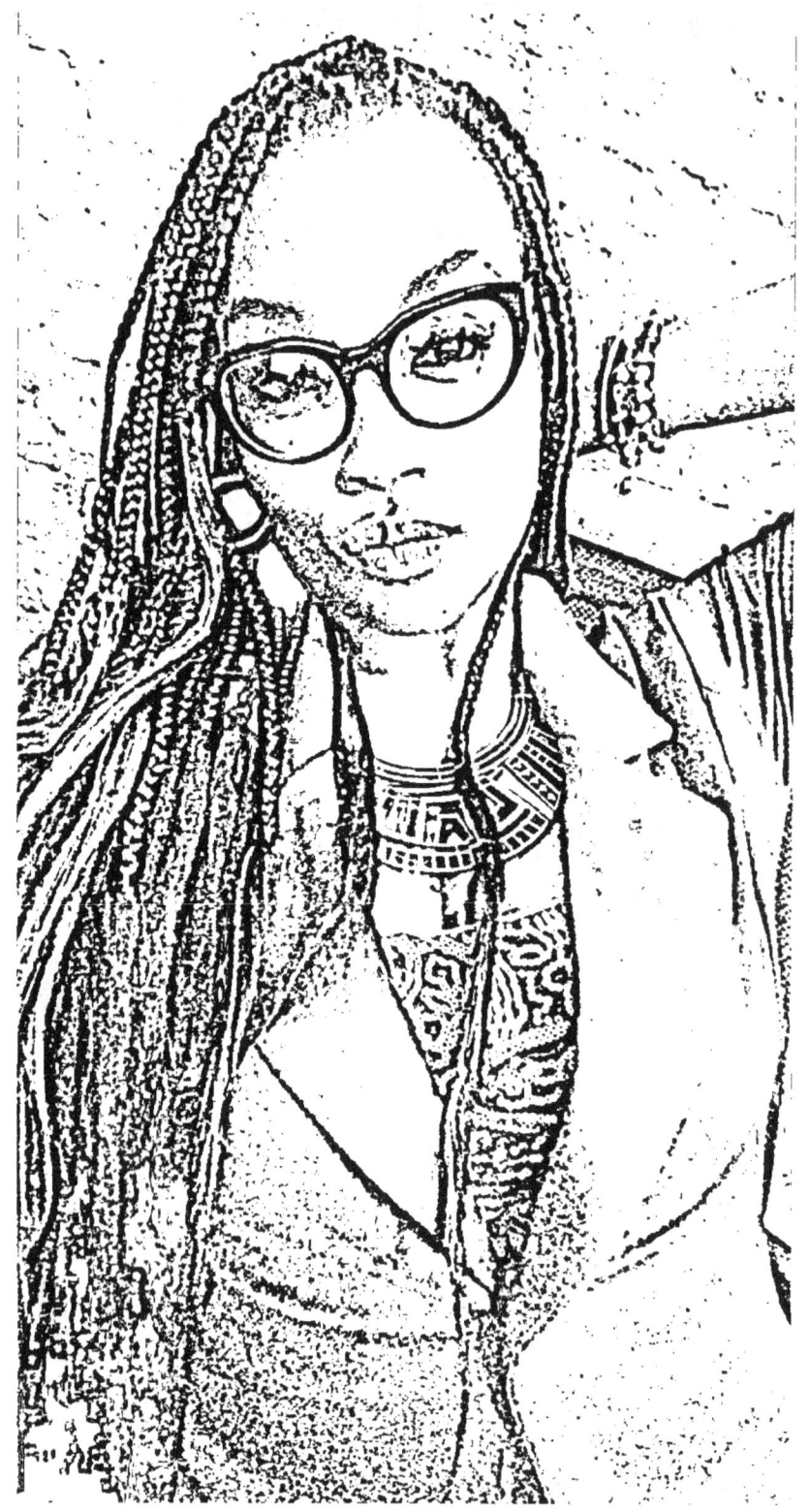

"Success is liking yourself, liking what you do, and liking how you do it." - Maya Angelou

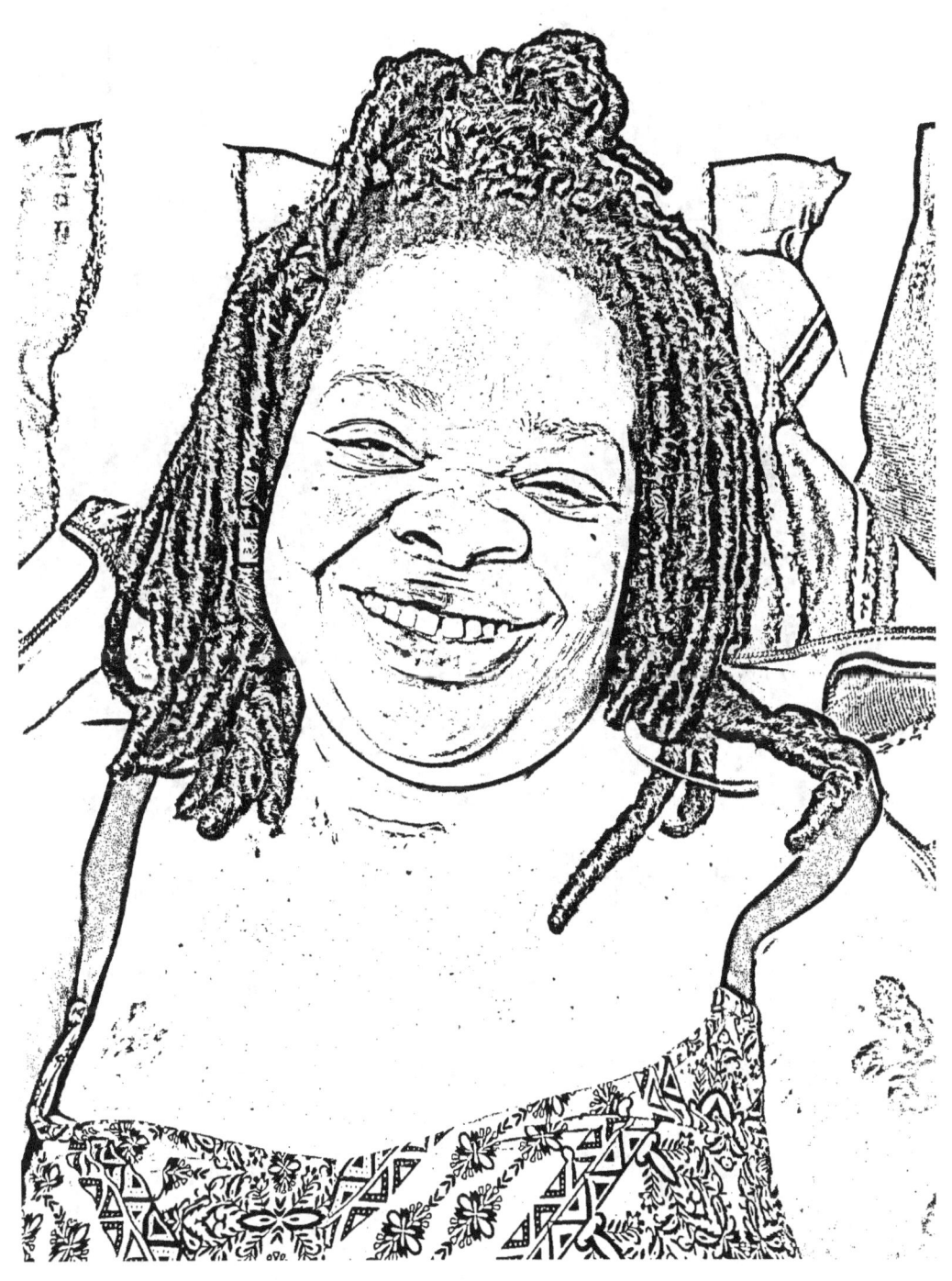

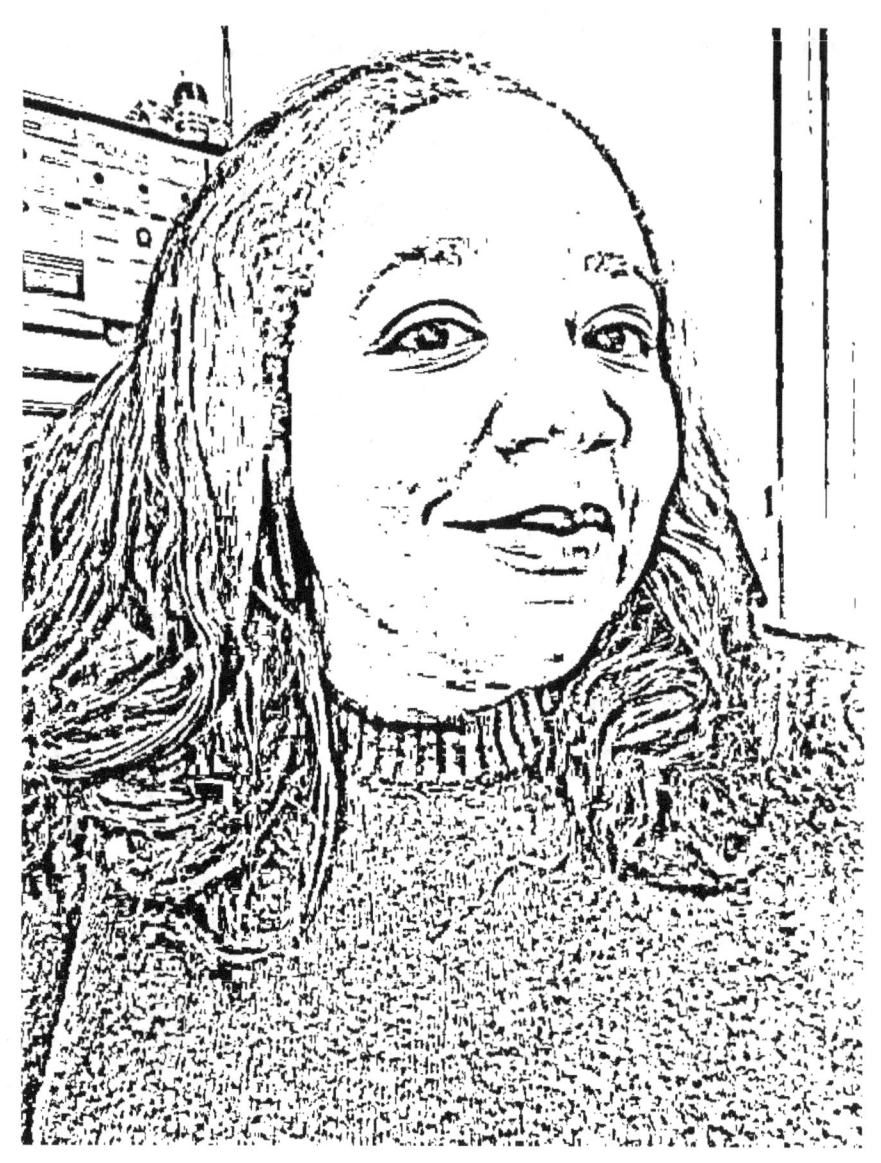

"I don't have to go around trying to save everybody anymore; that's not my job."
-Jada Pinkett Smith

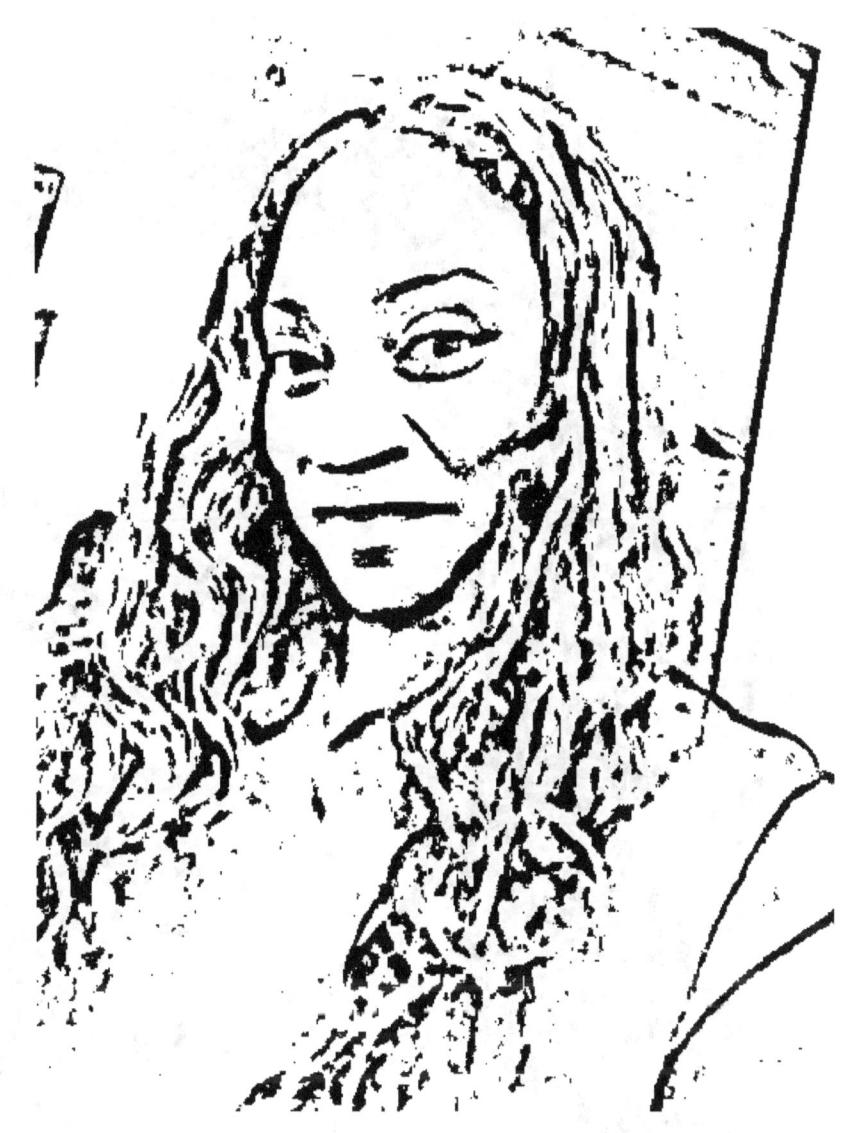

"You are the designer of your destiny; you are the author of your story."
– Lisa Nichols

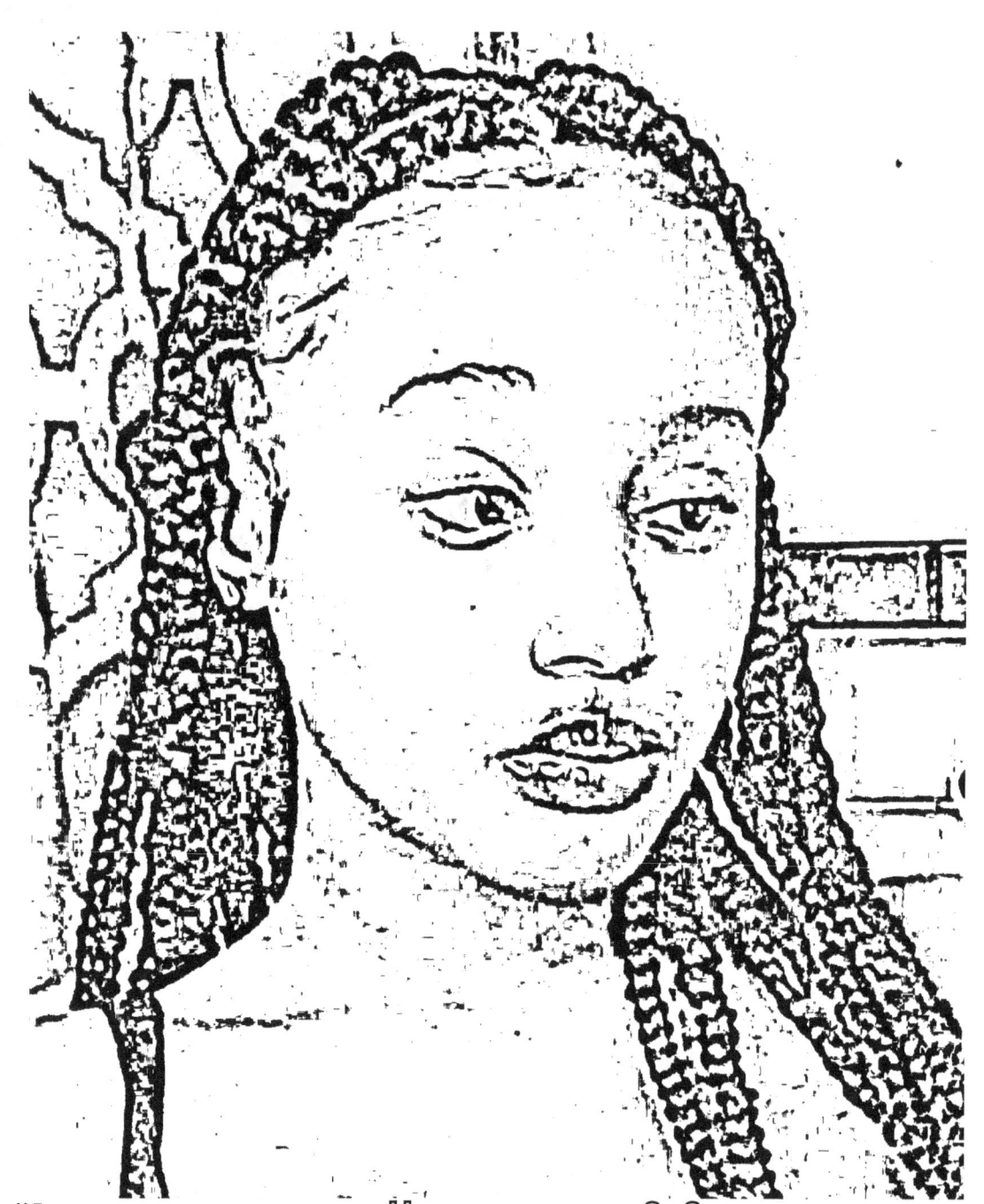

"Love is an endless act of forgiveness. Forgiveness is me giving up the right to hurt you for hurting me."
- Beyonce

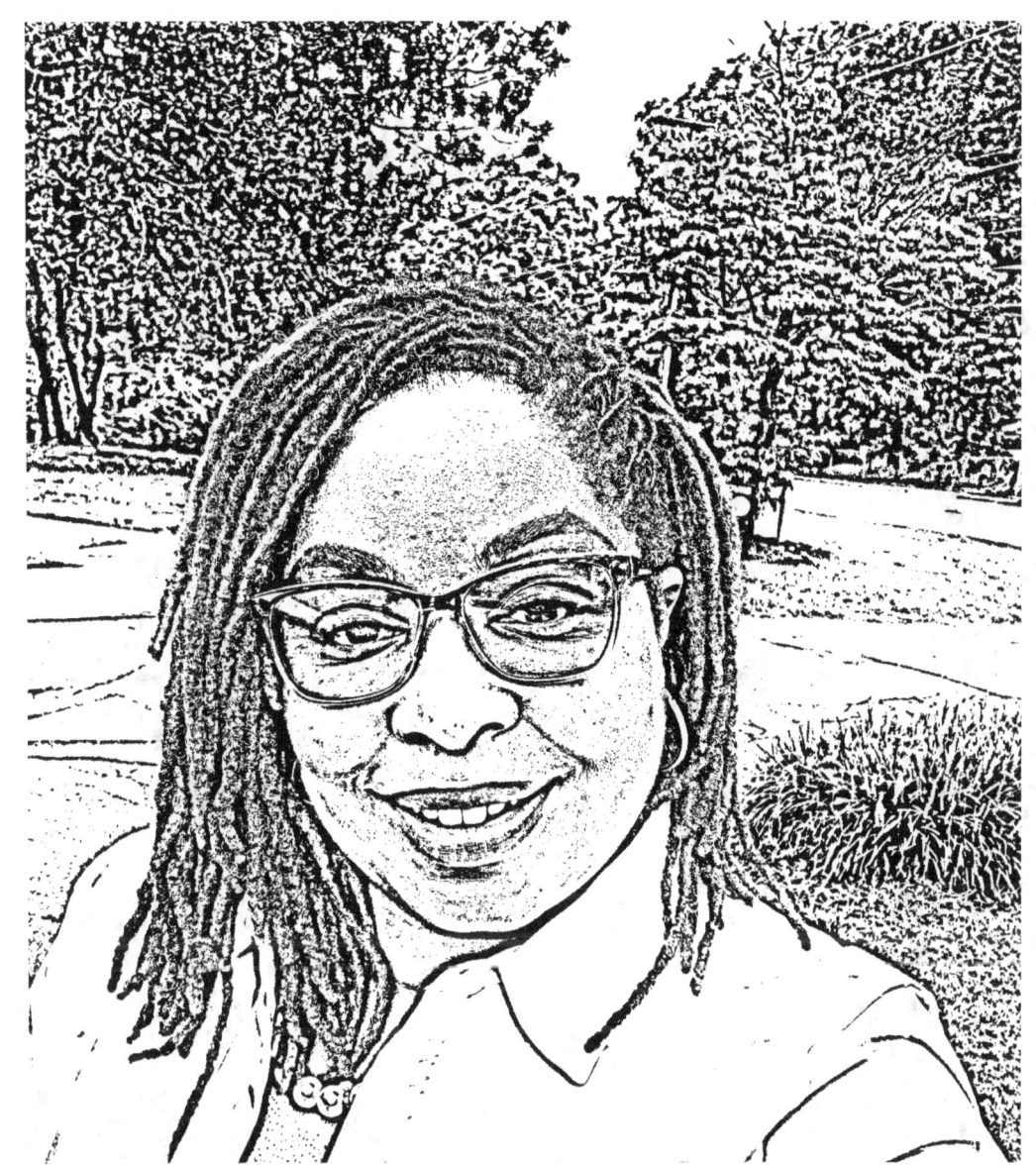

"It is better to look ahead and prepare than to look back and regret."
– Jackie Joyner-Kersee

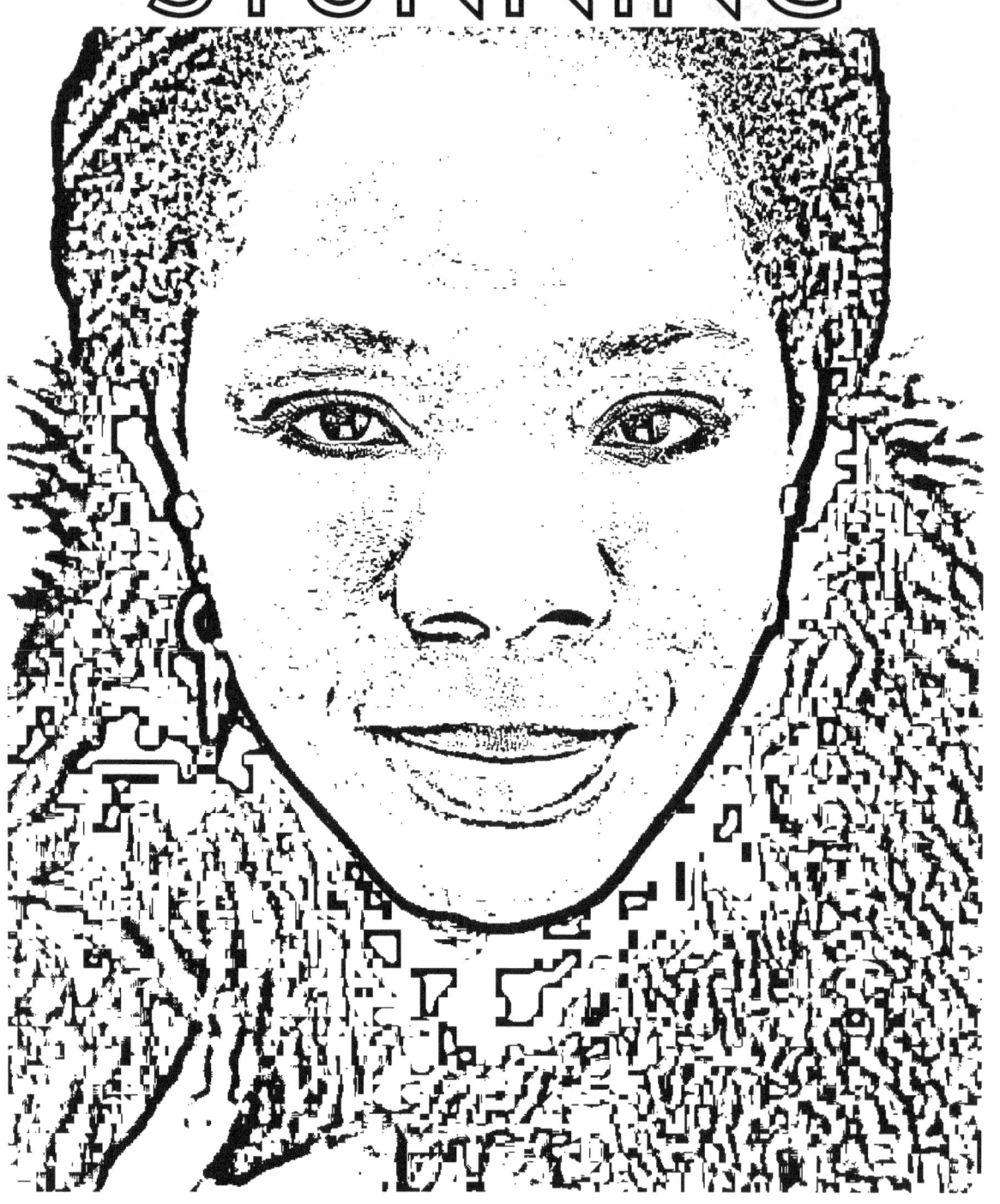

Curls Poppin'

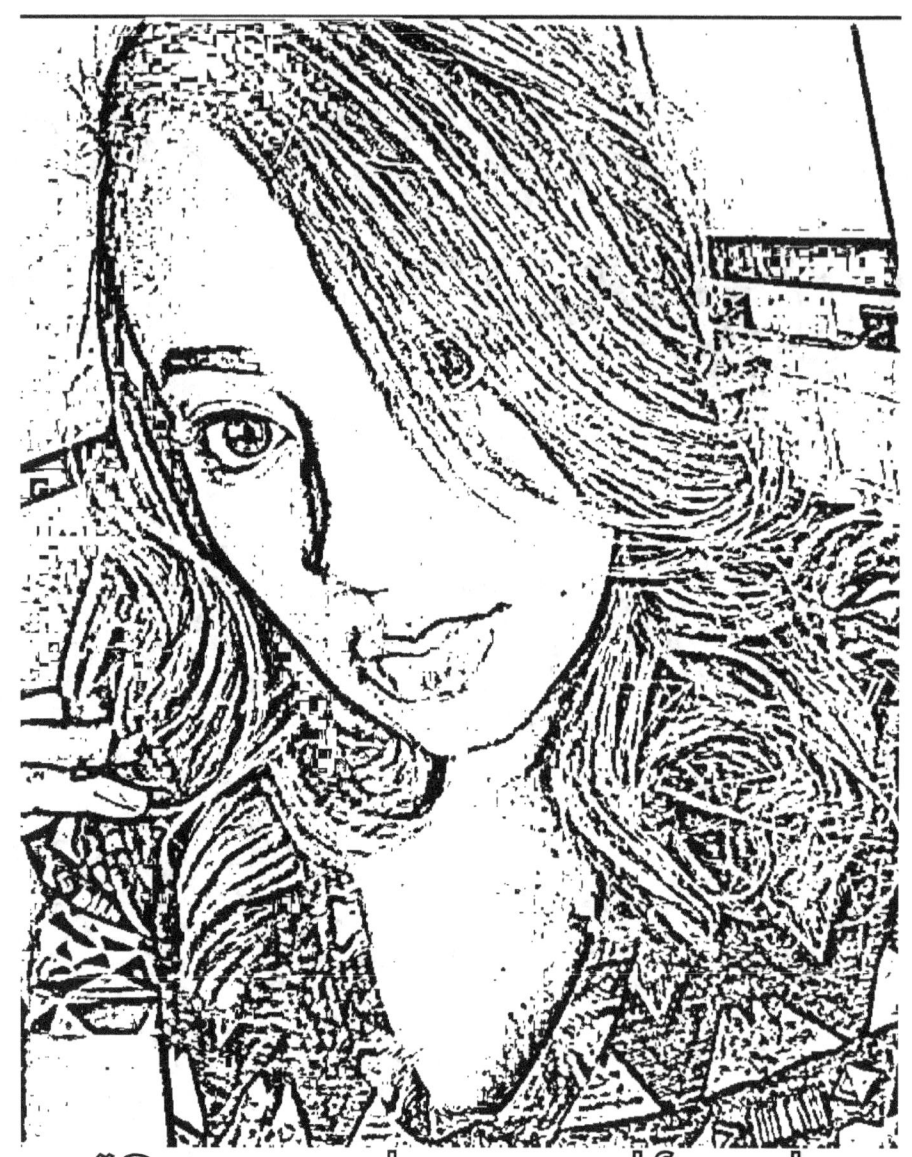

"Doing the best at this moment puts you in the best place for the next moment."– Oprah Winfrey

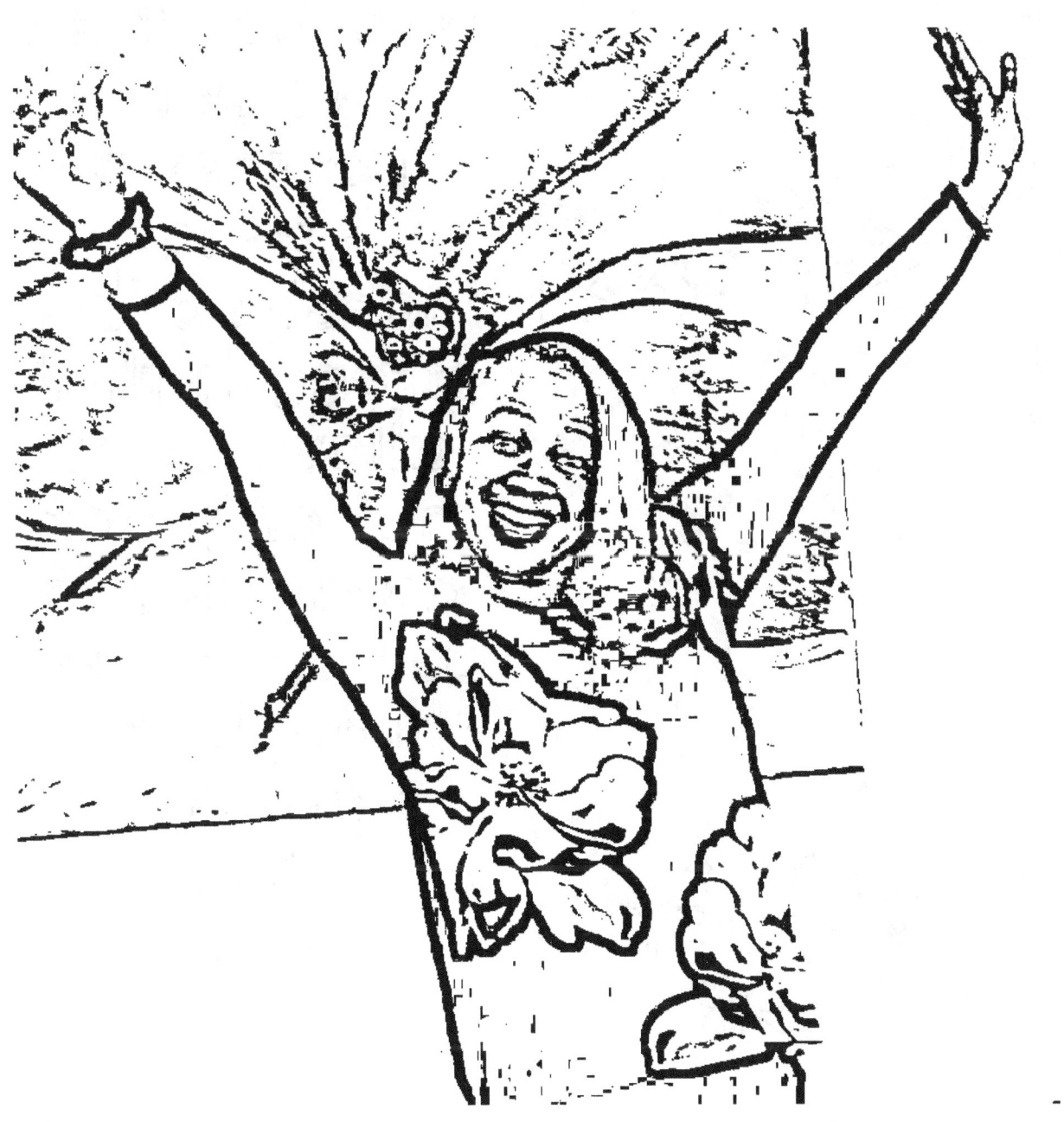

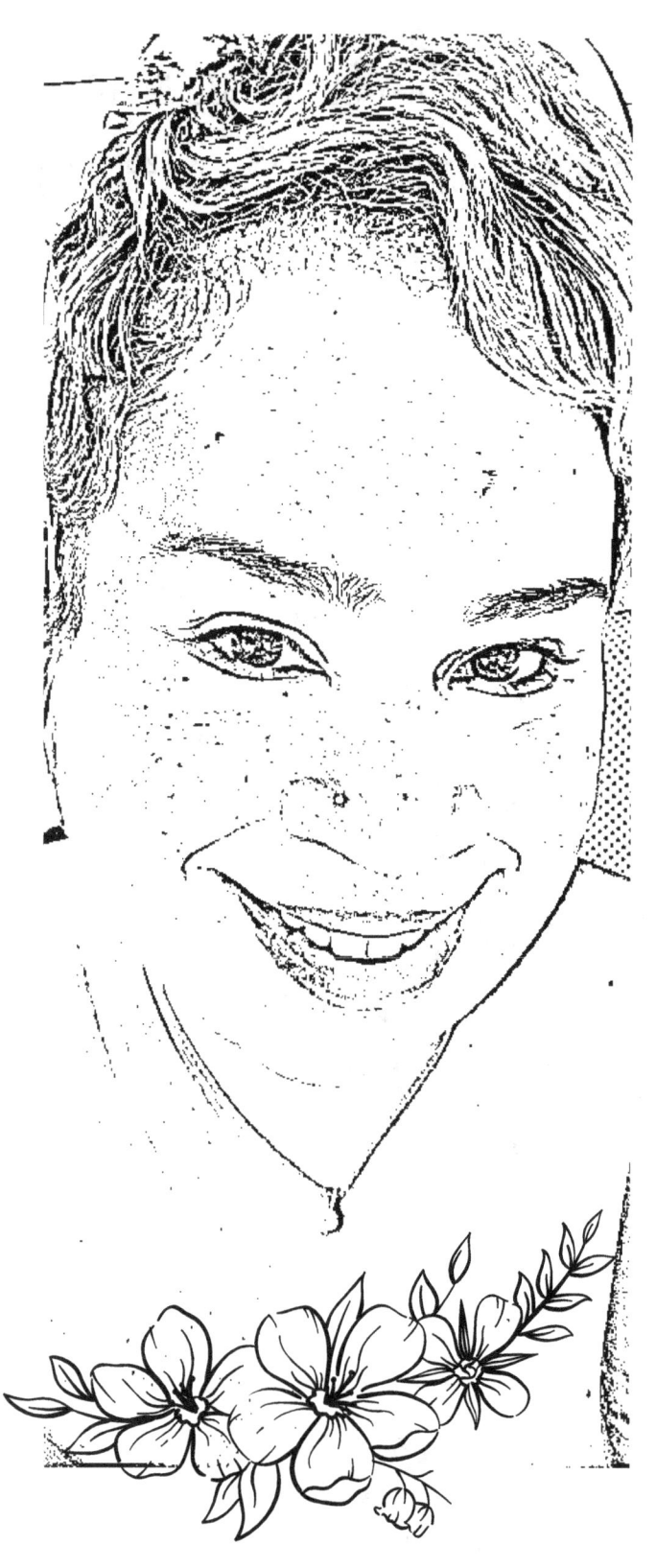

"I'm convinced that we Black women possess a special indestructible strength that allows us to not only get down, but to get up, to get through, and to get over."
— Janet Jackson

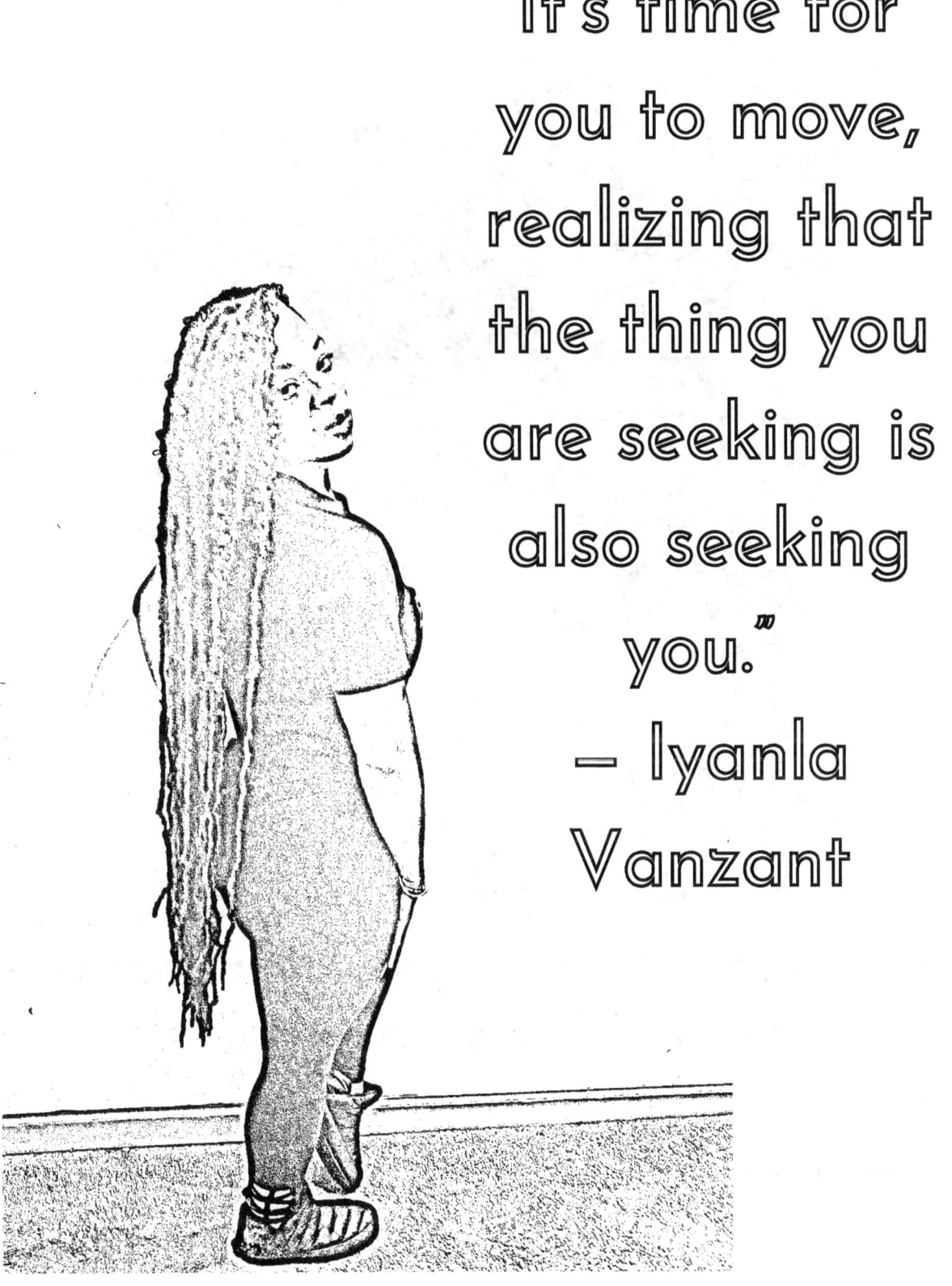

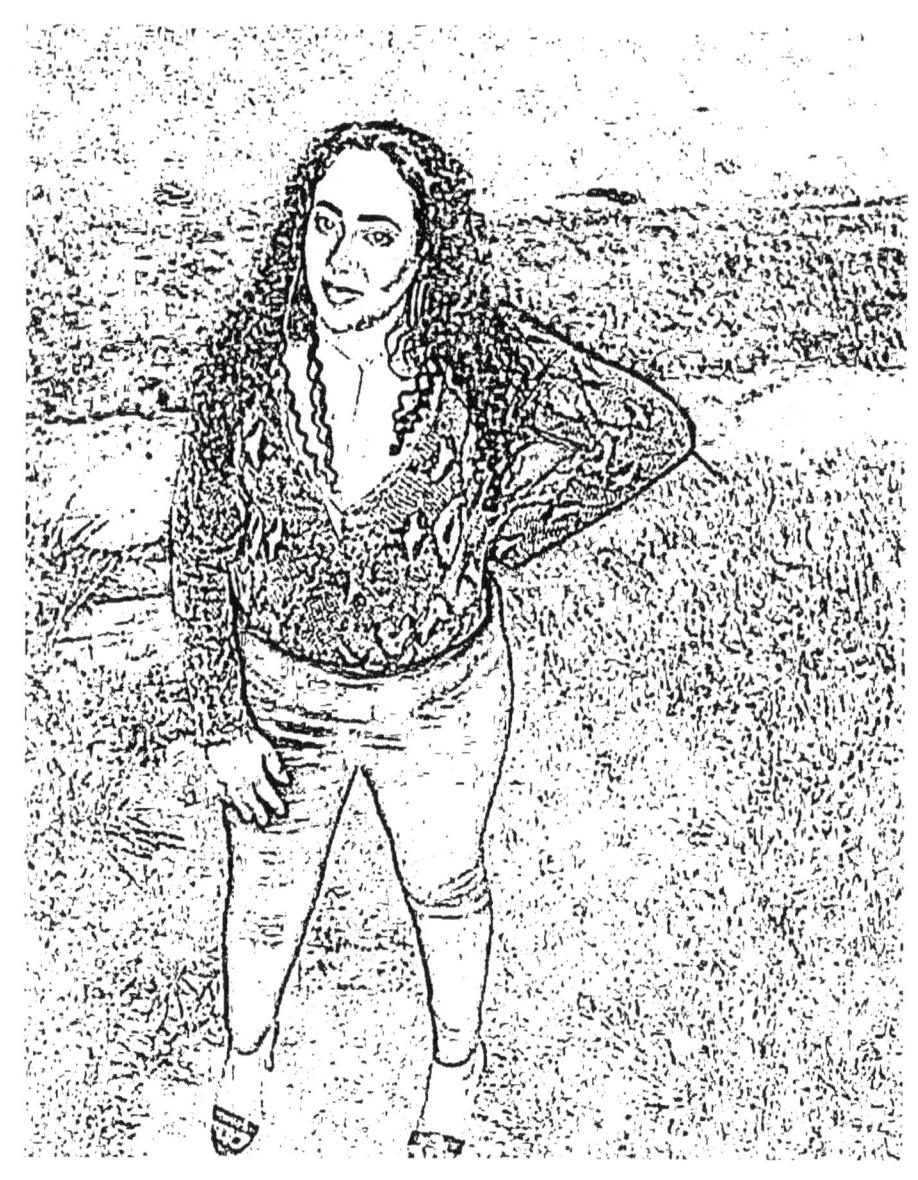

"Every great dream begins with a dreamer. Always remember, you have within you the strength, the patience, and the passion to reach for the stars to change the world."
-Harriet Tubman

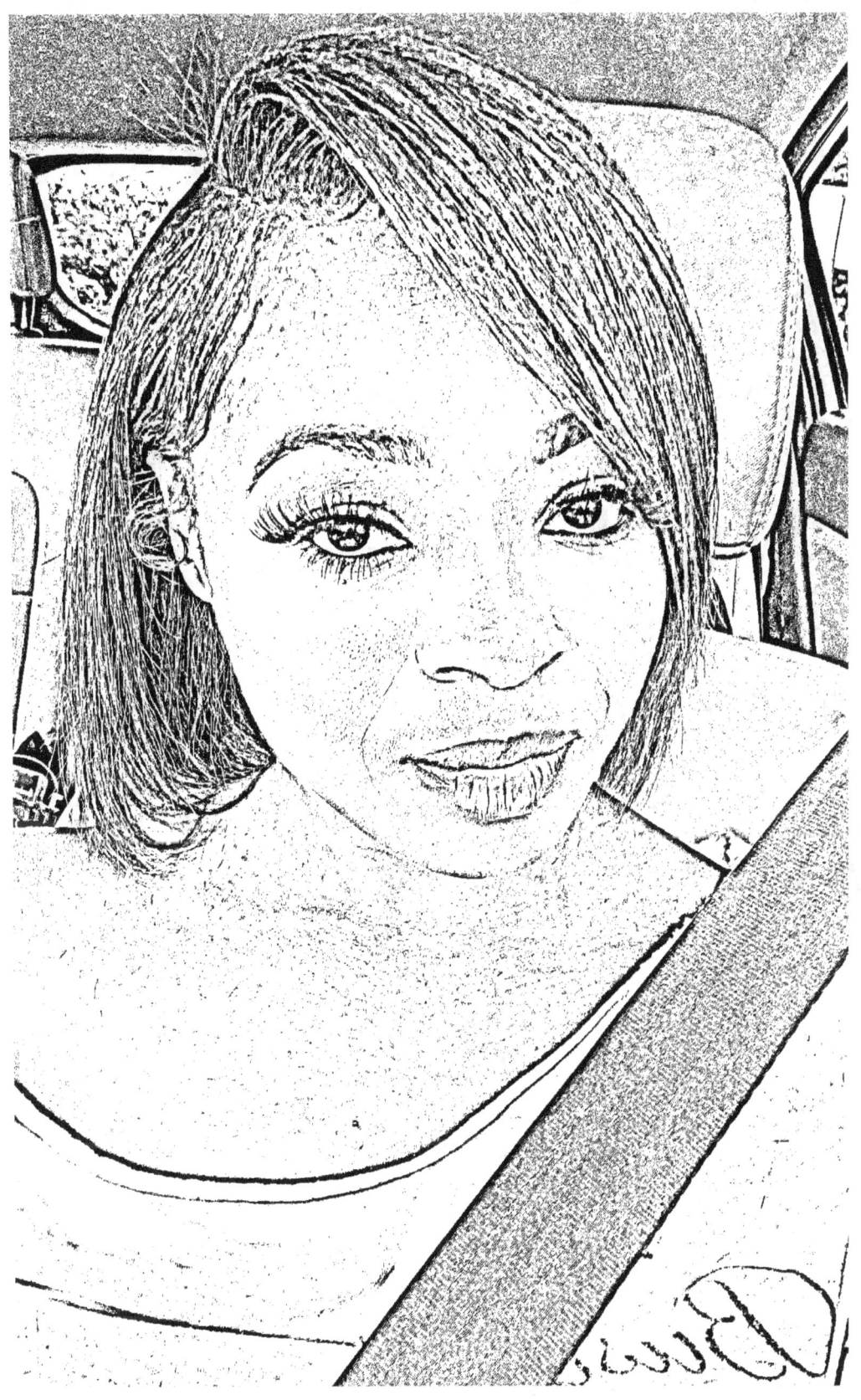

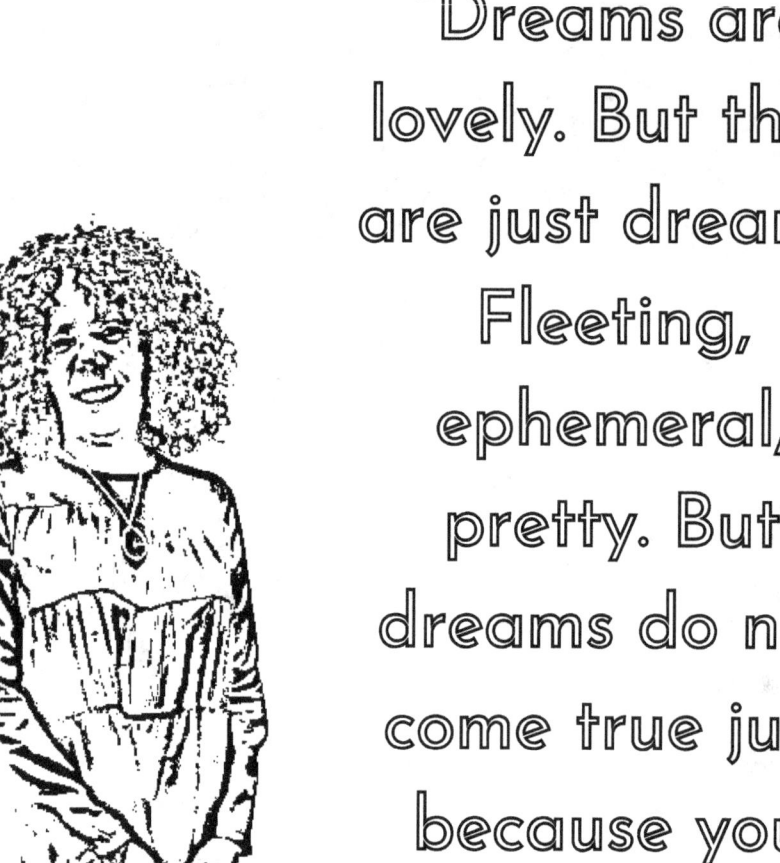

"Dreams are lovely. But they are just dreams. Fleeting, ephemeral, pretty. But dreams do not come true just because you dream them. It's hard work that makes things happen. It's hard work that creates change."
- Shonda Rhimes

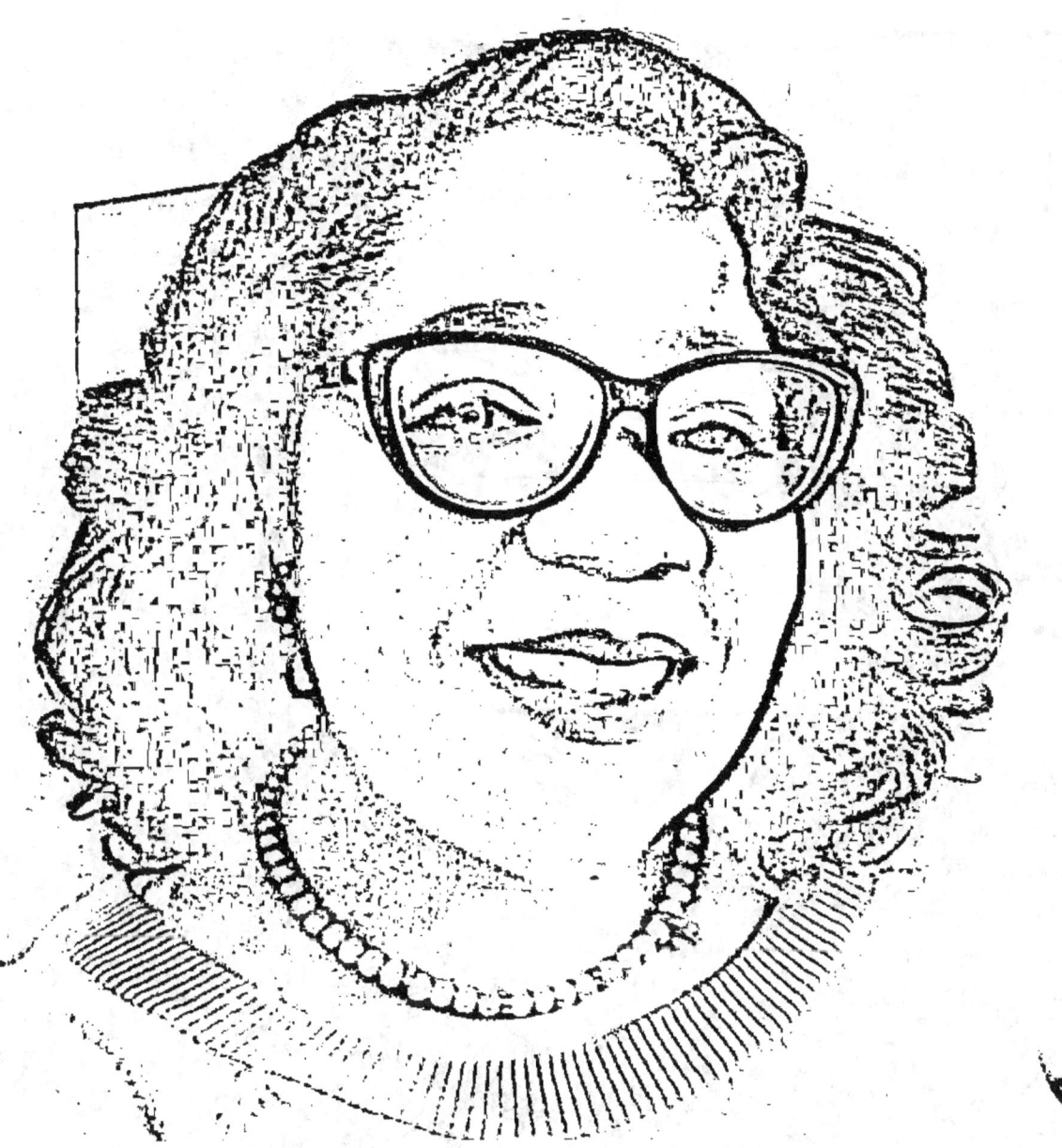

"If you are silent about your pain, they'll kill you and say you enjoyed it."
– Zora Neale Hurston

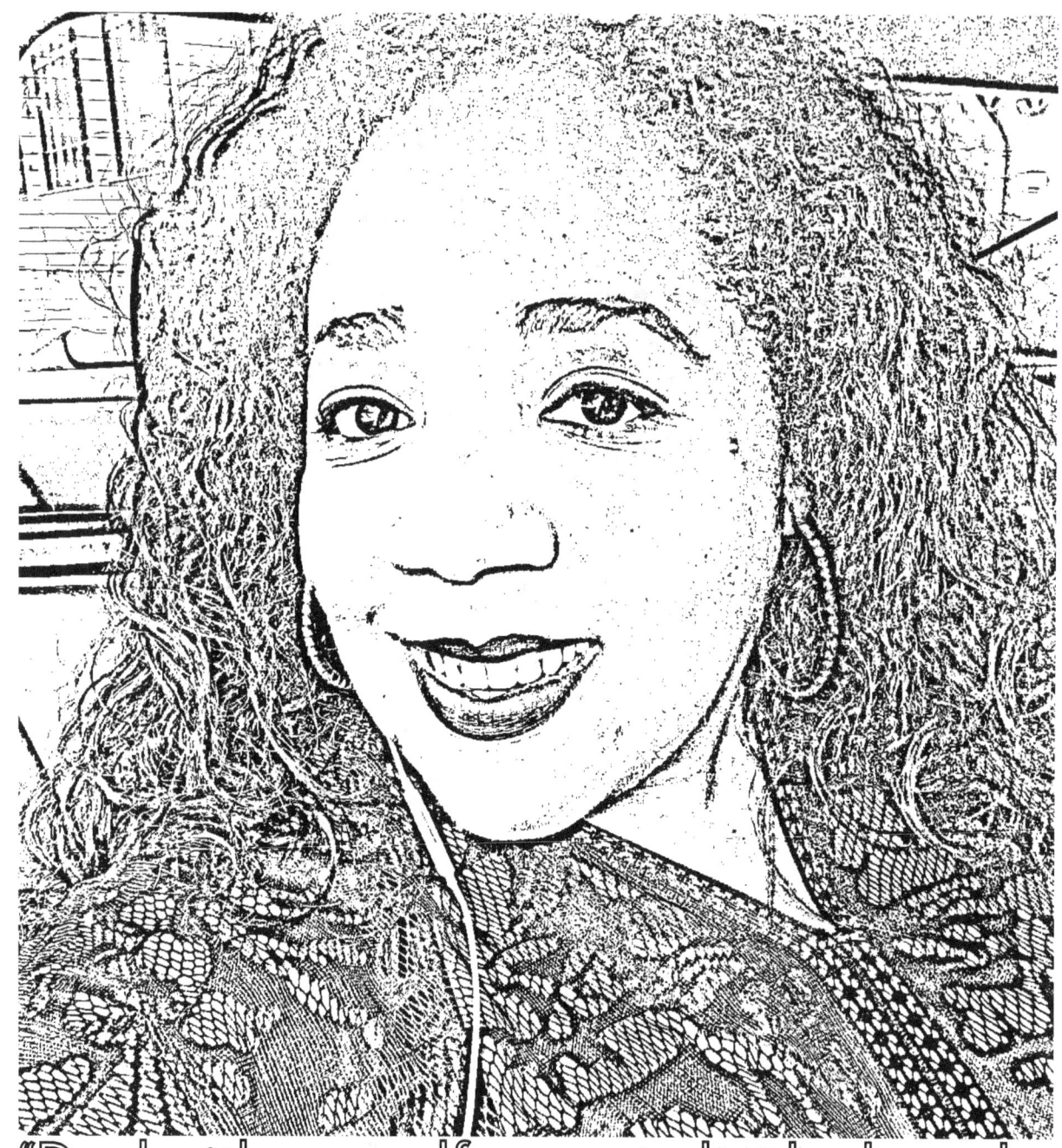

"Deal with yourself as an individual worthy of respect, and make everyone else deal with you the same way."
- Nikki Giovanni

"Caring for myself is not self-indulgence, it is self-preservation, and that is an act of political warfare.
—Audre Lorde

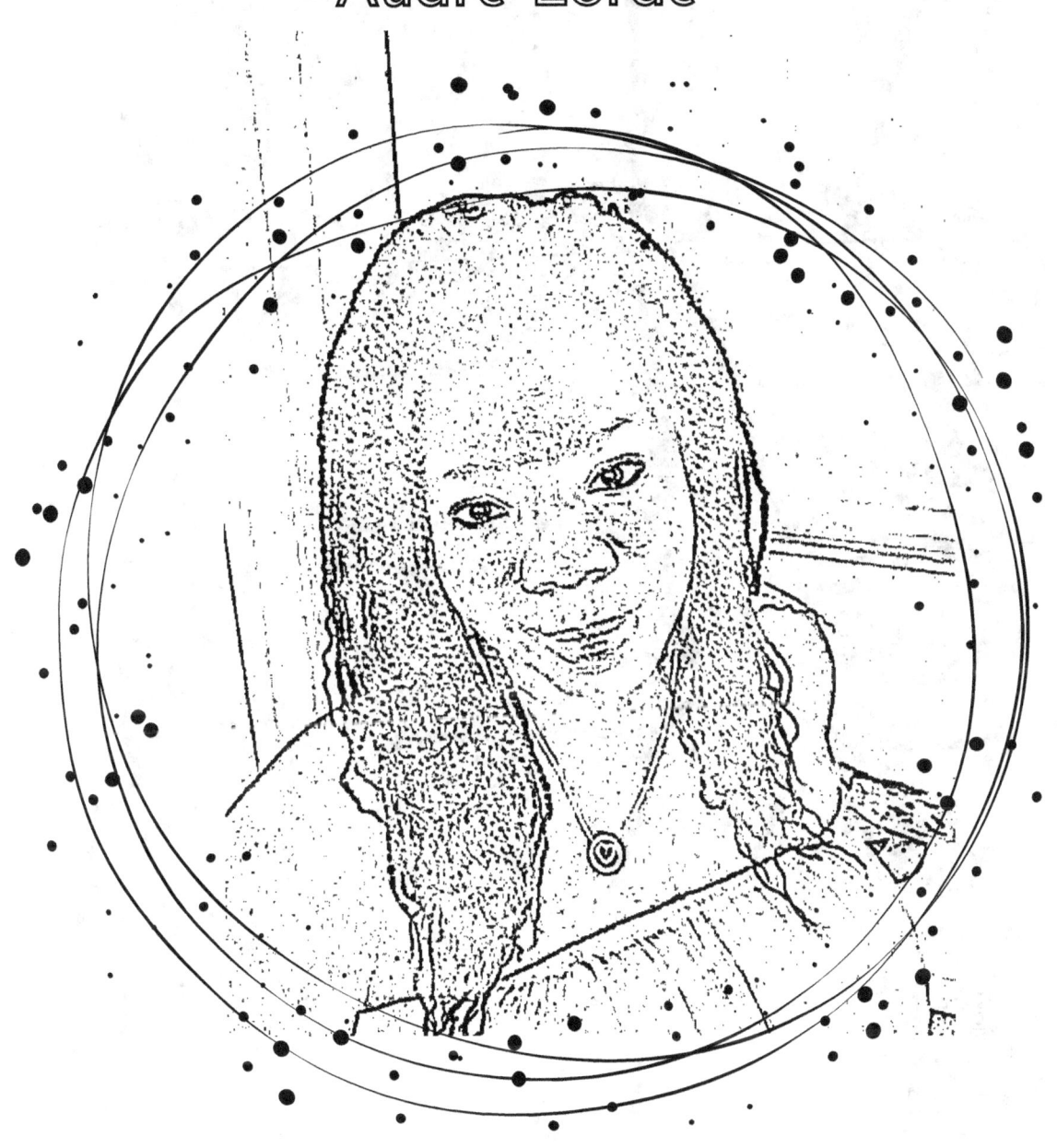

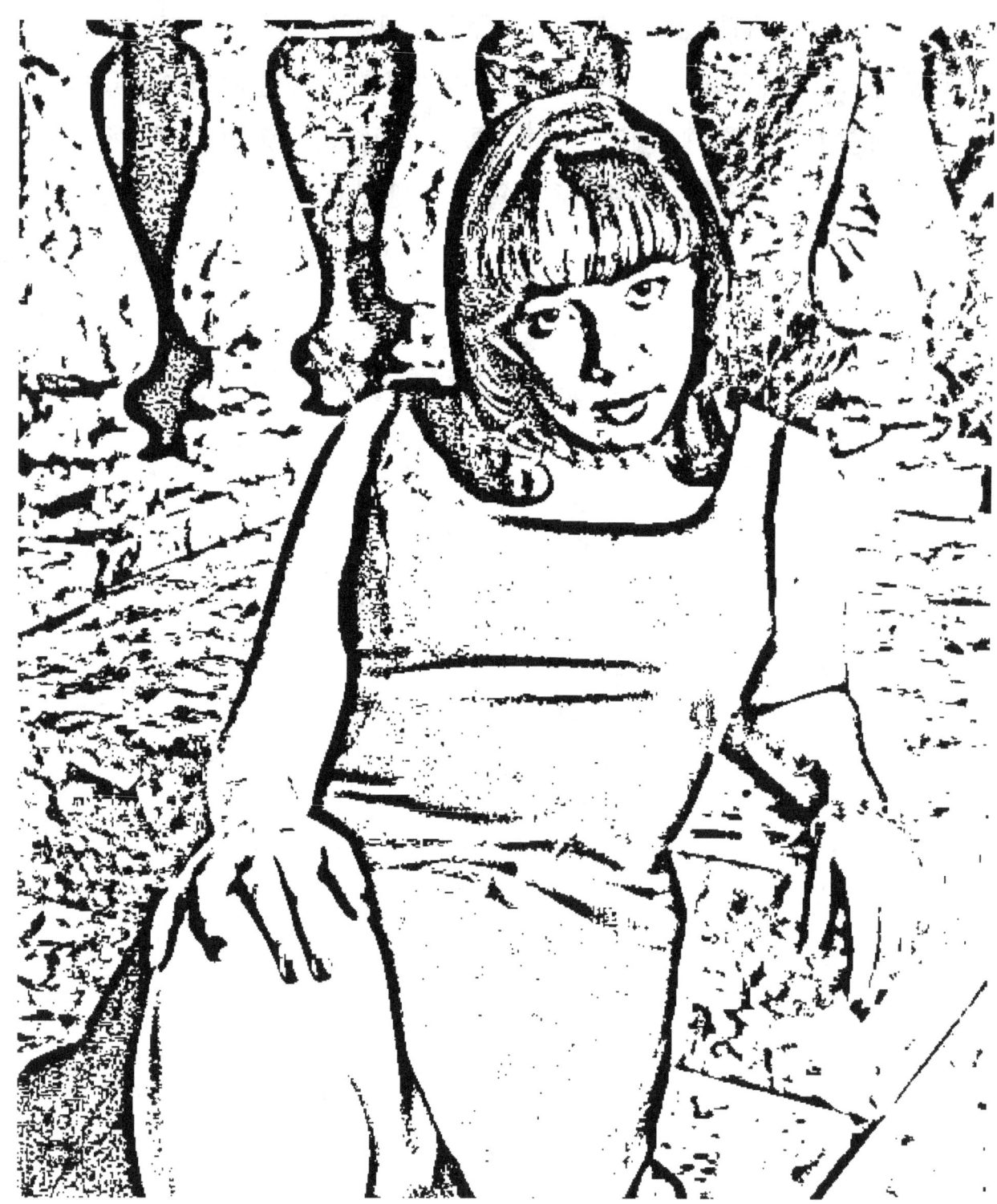

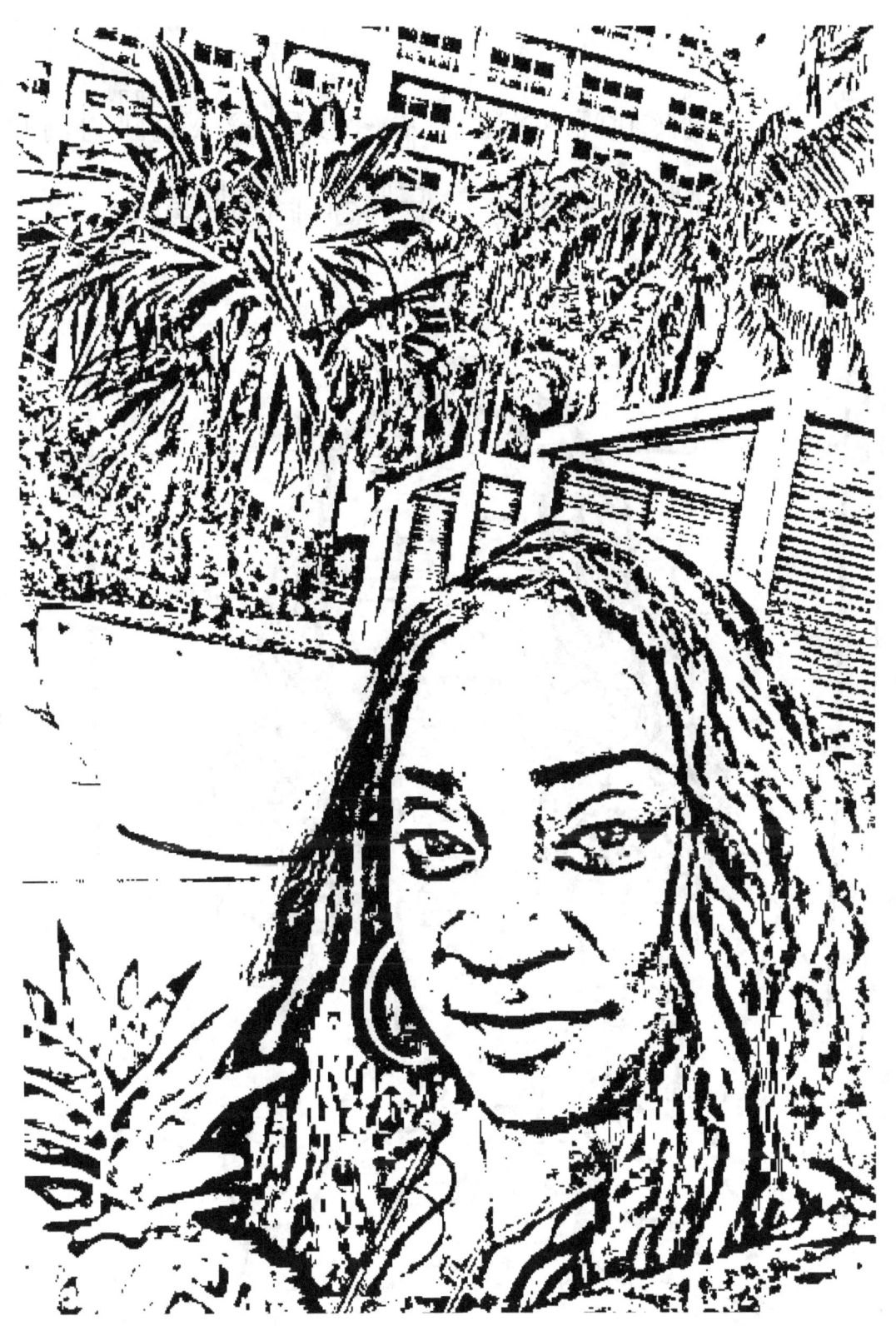

"Give light and people will find the way." Ella Baker

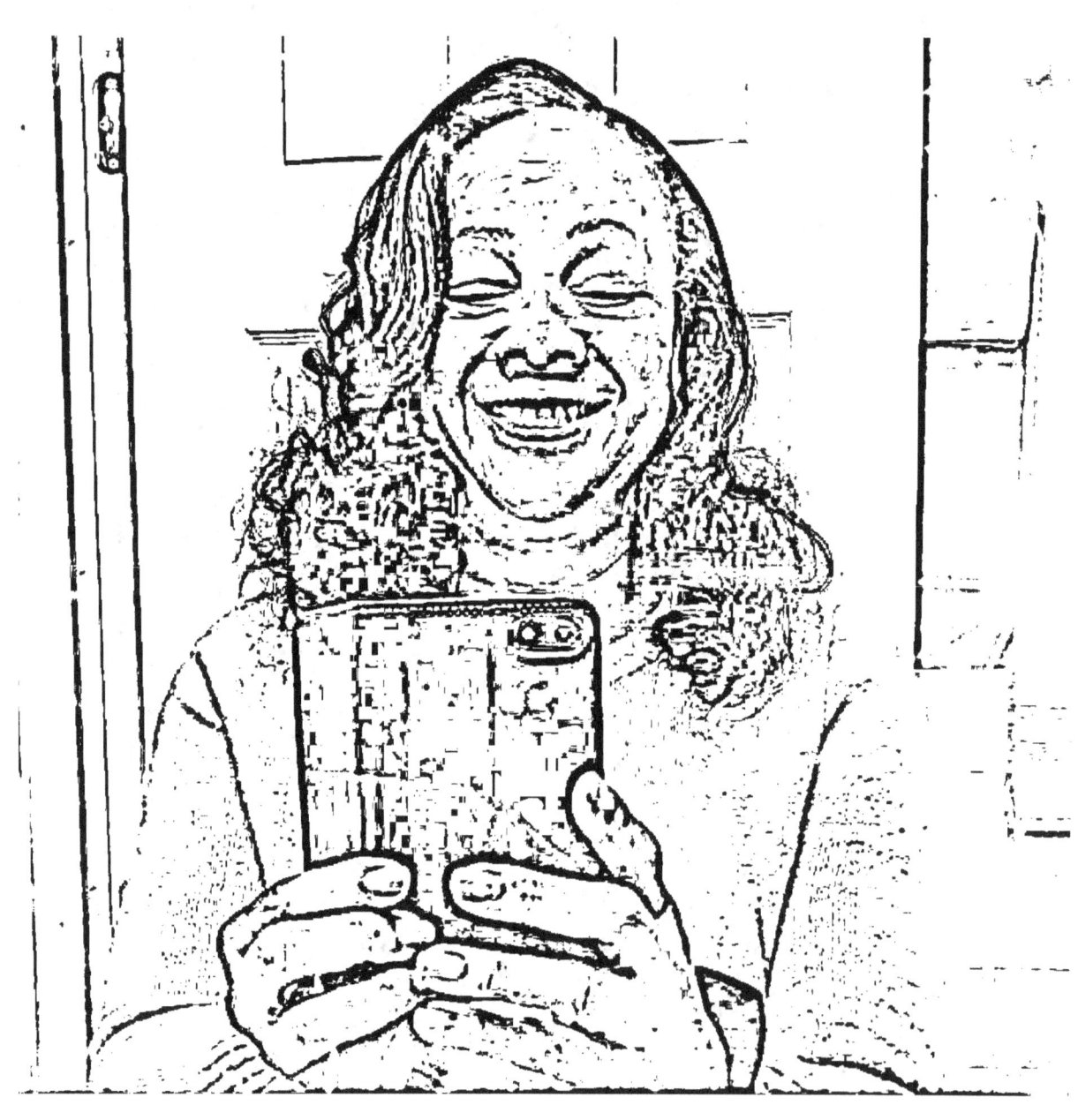

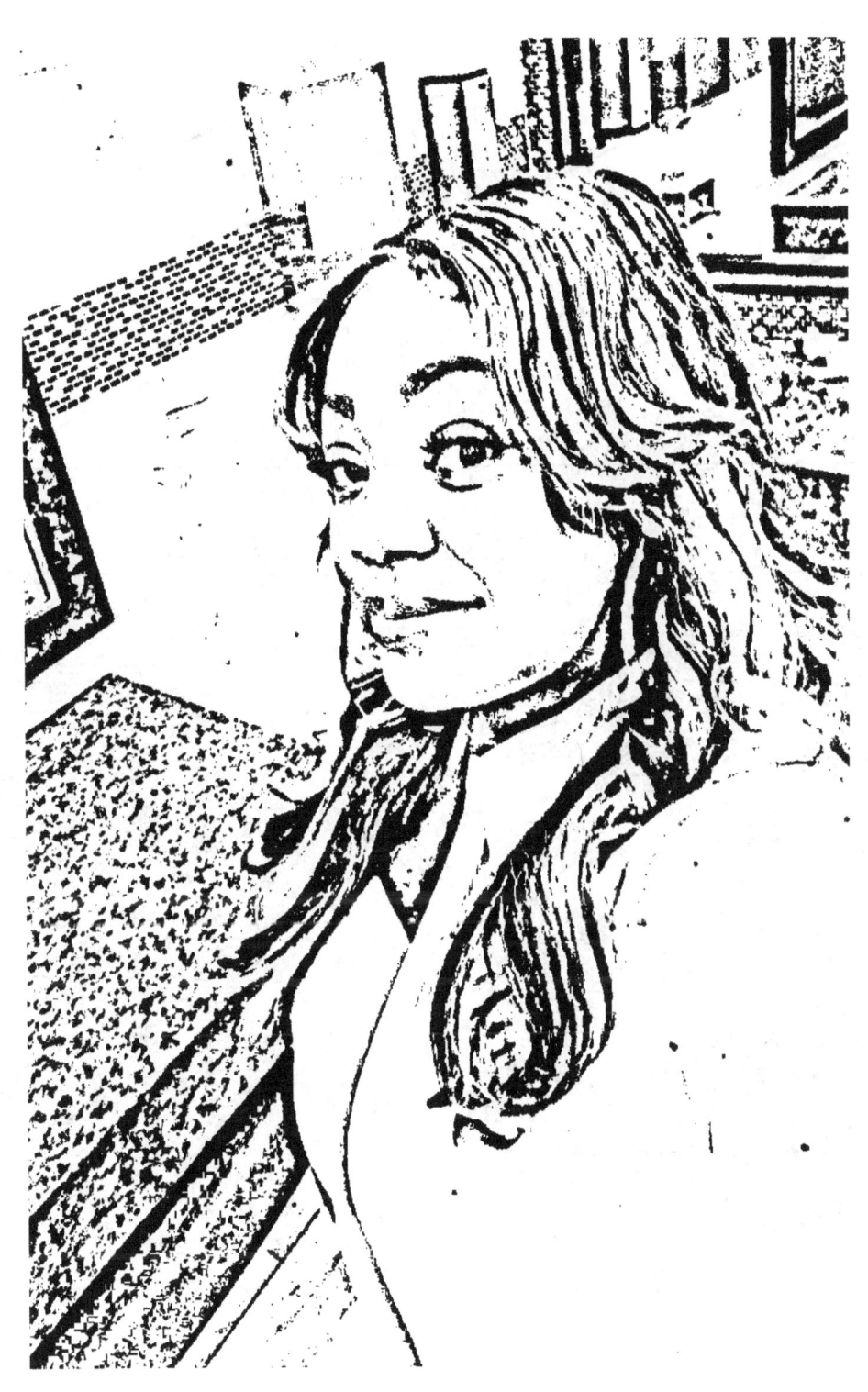

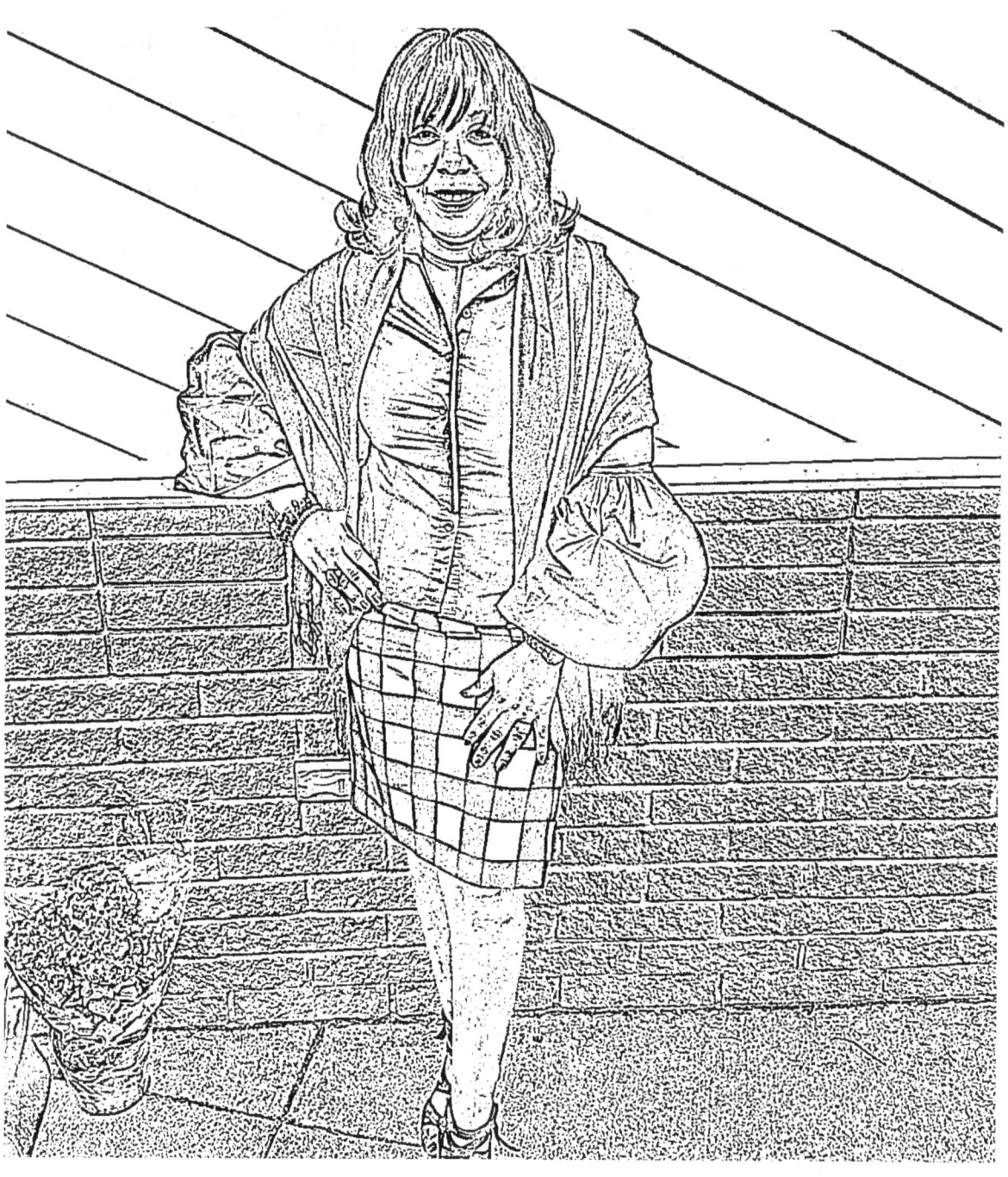

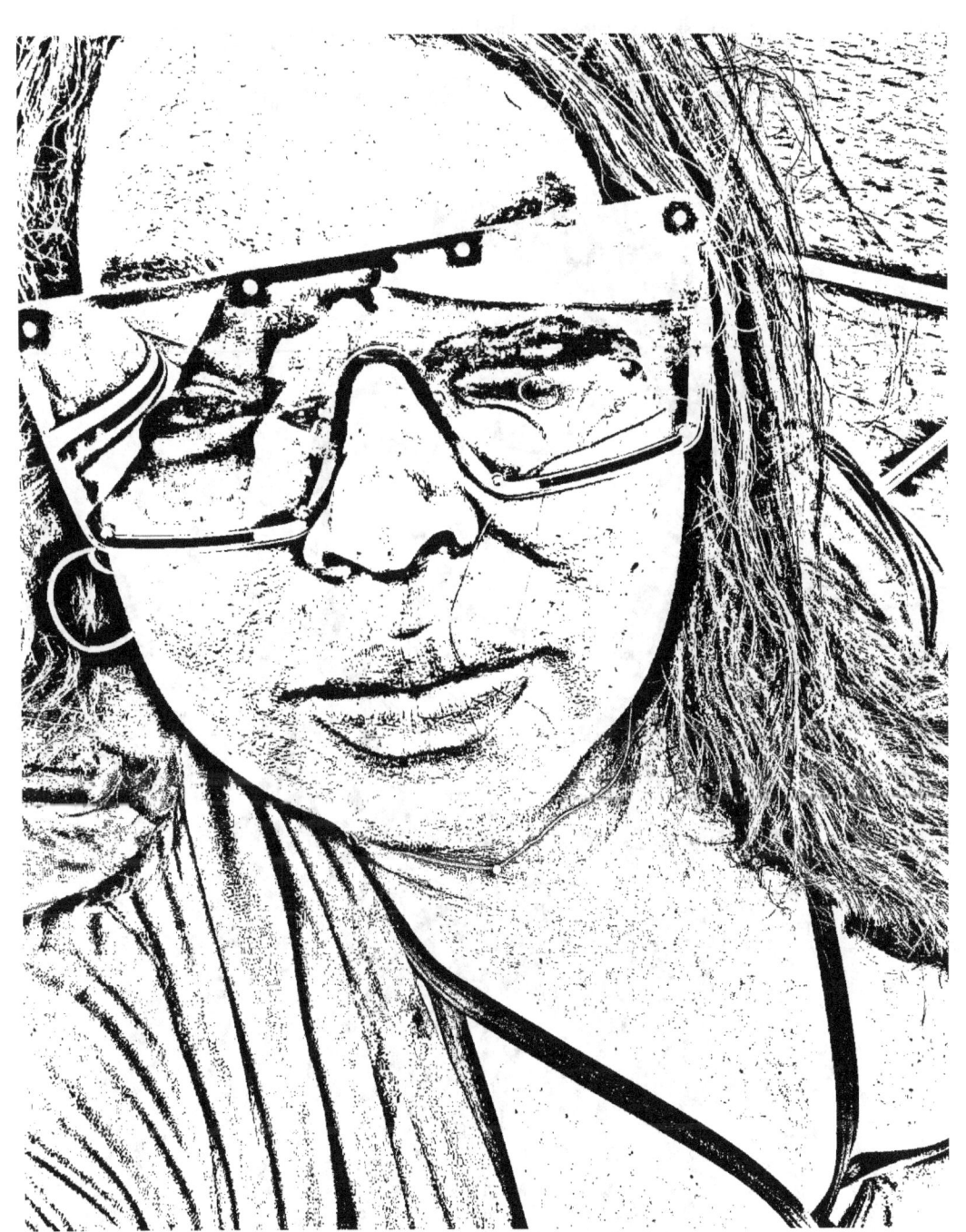

"Breathe. Let go. And remind yourself that this very moment is the only one you know you have for sure." - Oprah Winfrey

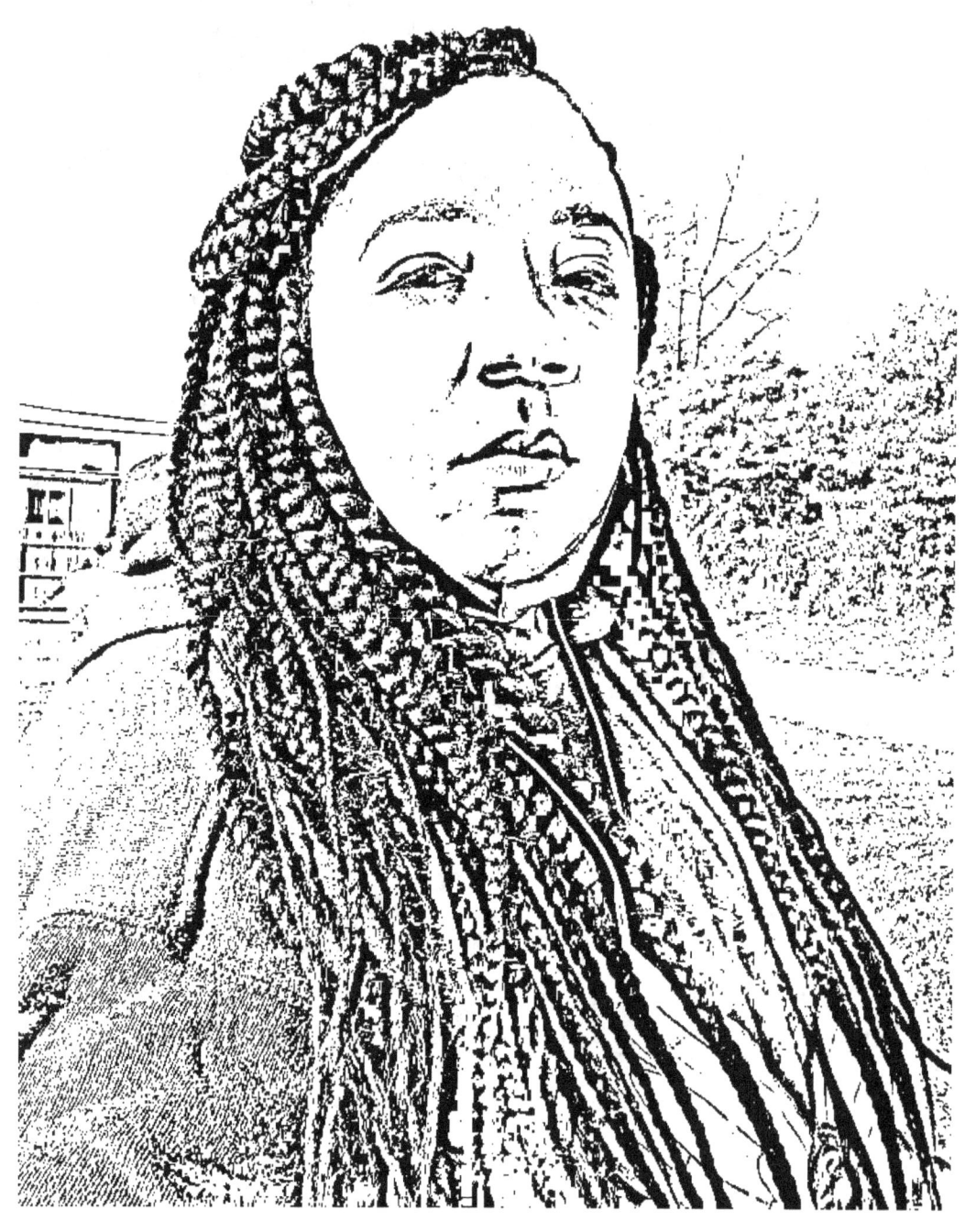

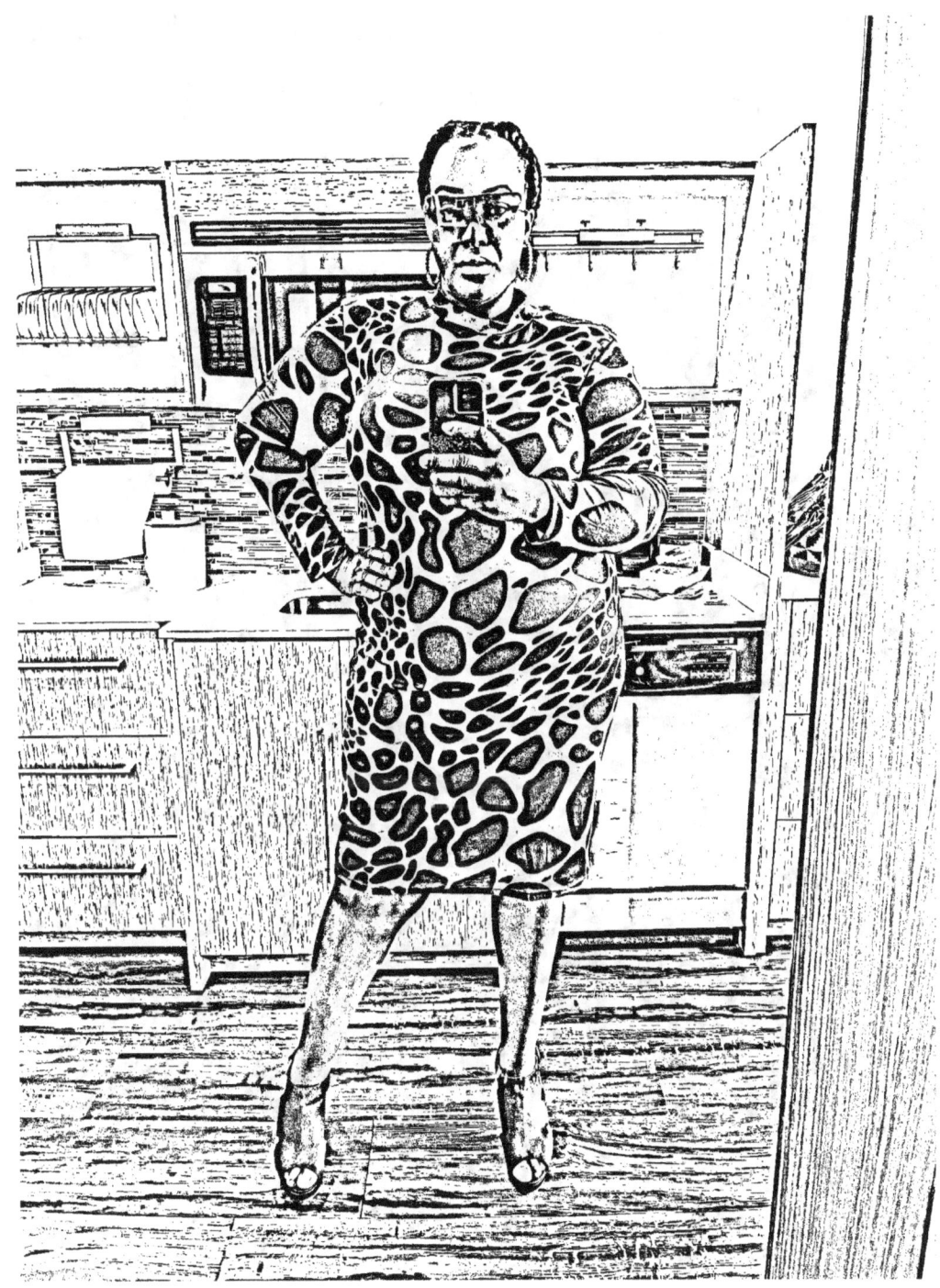

"We must let go of the life we have planned... to accept the one that is waiting for us." -Joseph Campbell

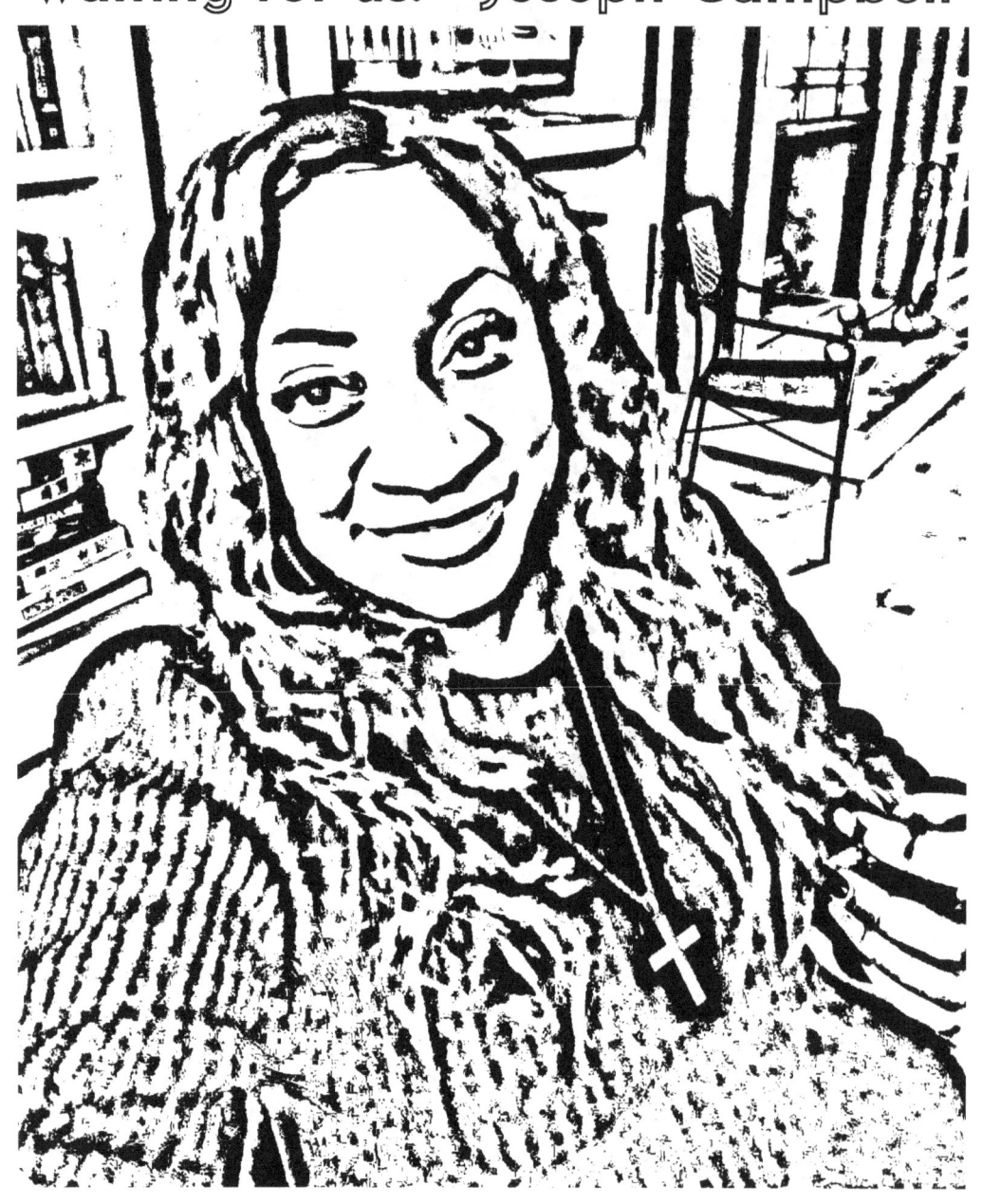

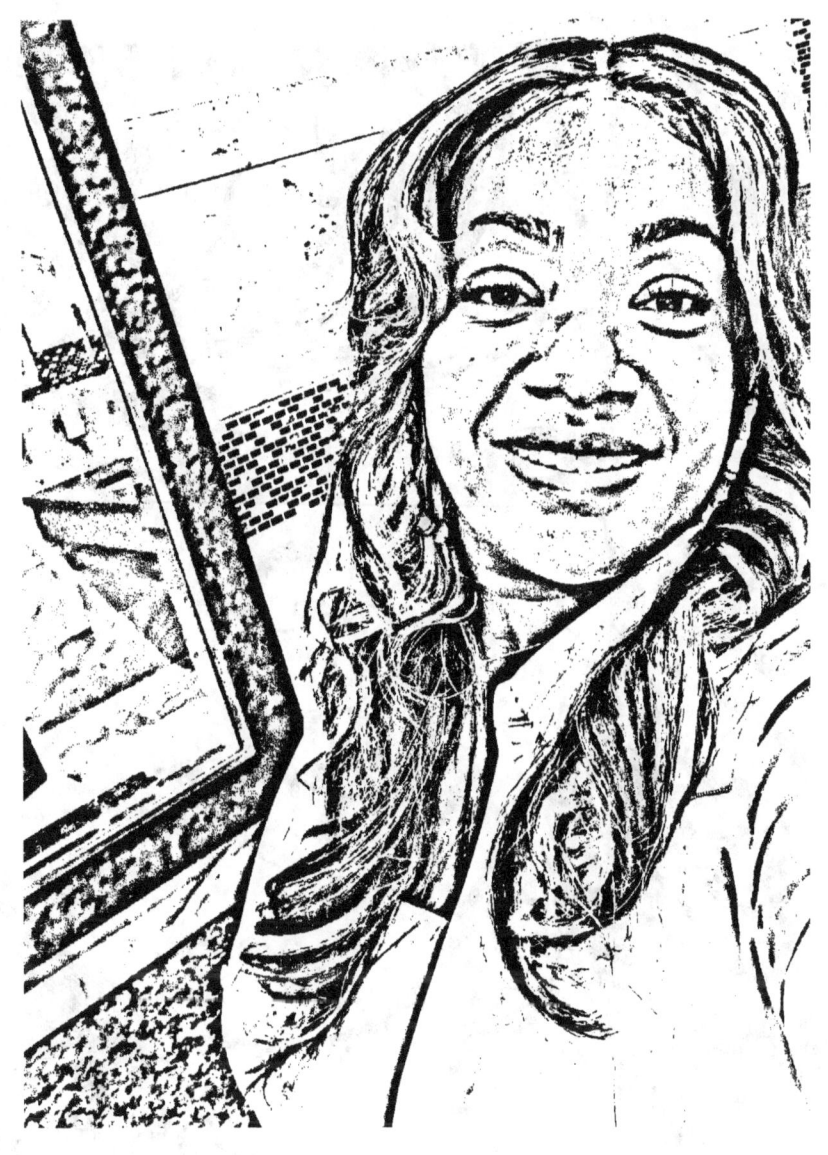

"You are on the eve of a complete victory. You can't go wrong. The world is behind you." - Josephine Baker

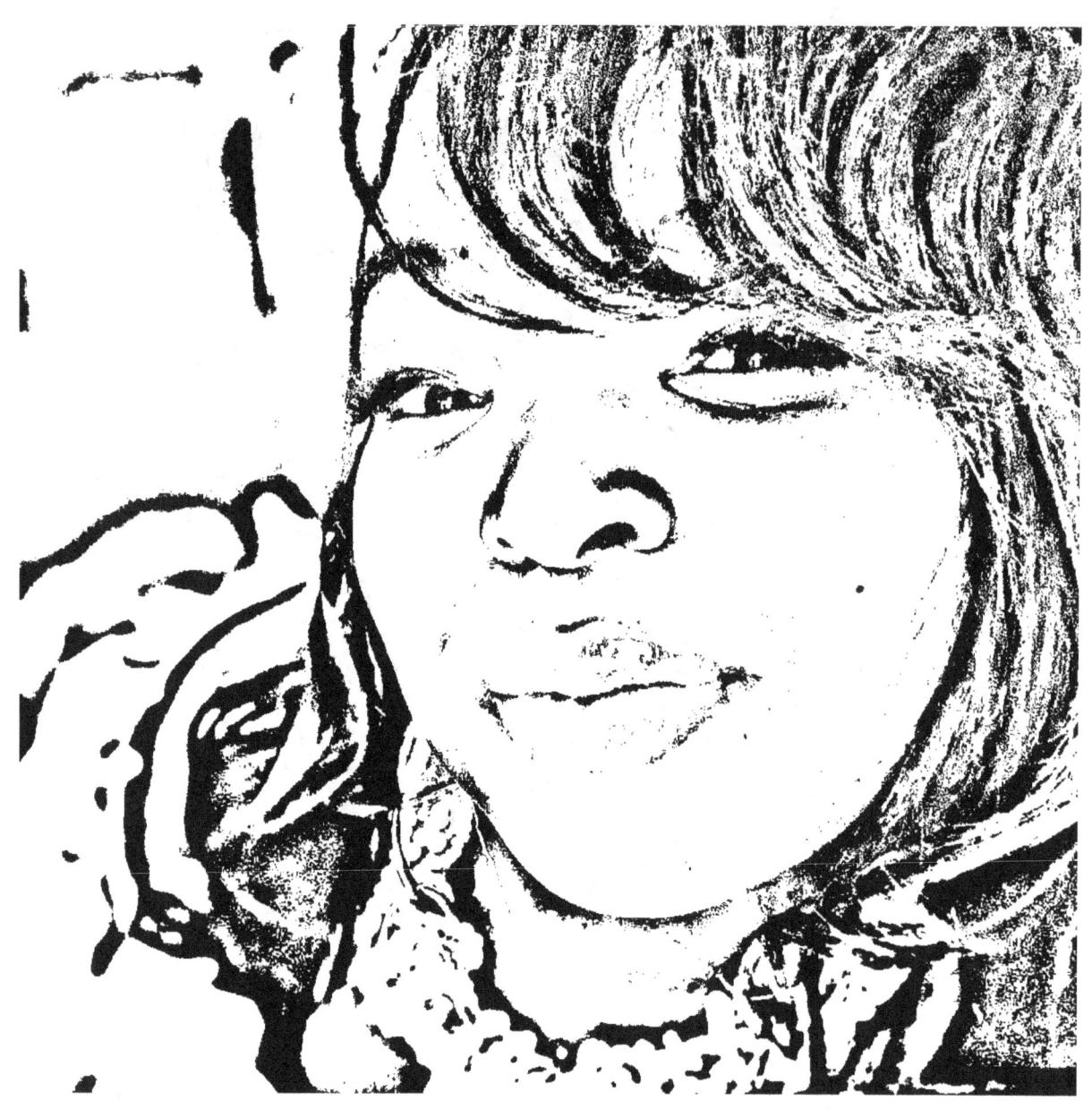

"My mission in life is not merely to survive, but to thrive; and to do so with some passion, some compassion, some humor, and some style."
— Maya Angelou

Special Thanks to the beautiful black women featured in this book

Loretta - Devan - Brenda - Kelly - Willetrea - Ebony - April - Tanita - Christal - Pheonicia - Vernita - Davida - Stephanie - Anne - Angelena - Cheriees - Angela - Staci - Latoya - Micah - Simone - Keana

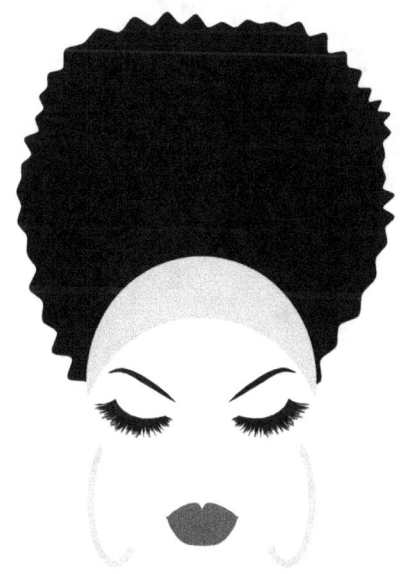

www.ingramcontent.com/pod-product-compliance
Lightning Source LLC
Chambersburg PA
CBHW080528220526
45465CB00006B/2634